99 Things You Wish You Knew Before®... Choosing Adoption

Your easy-to-read guide to adoption

Robert A. Kasky, Esq.

Jeffrey A. Kasky, Esq.

www.99-series.com

The 99 Series, LLC
85 N. Main Street
Florida, NY 10921
646-233-4366

The authors have done their best to present accurate and up-to-
date information in this book, but they cannot guarantee that the
information is correct or will suit your particular situation.

Disclaimer: All characters appearing in this work are fictitious.
Any resemblance to real persons, living or dead, is purely
coincidental.

Limit of Liability and Disclaimer of Warranty: The publisher has
used its best efforts in preparing this book, and the information
provided herein is provided "as is."

First published by The 99 Series 2012

Ginger Marks Cover design and Layout
DocUmeantDesigns, www.DocUmeantDesigns.com

Philip S Marks Editor

Distributed by DocUmeant Publishing
For inquiries about volume orders, please contact:
99 Book Series, Inc.
books@99-series.com

Library of Congress Cataloging-in-Publication Data
Kasky, Robert A & Kasky, Jeffrey A
        99 Things You Wish You Knew Before
Choosing Adoption: adoption, adoptive parents, birth,
adoption law, domestic adoption, international
adoption, adoption home study.

LCCN - 2012949887

Printed in the United States Of America
ISBN-13: 978-1-937801-21-2 (paperback)
ISBN-10:1937801217

WORDS OF PRAISE

FOR...

---

99 Things You Wish You Knew Before®... Choosing Adoption

"Before retiring from the Circuit Court bench I had the distinct pleasure of seeing the Kaskys in court on a regular basis for years—sometimes as often as weekly while in the Family Court. Their book reflects the professionalism and knowledge they constantly displayed in court. This book simplifies a complex area of the law for the layperson and practitioner alike. These are the frequently asked questions, and then some, presented in an easy-to-understand and very entertaining format."

—John A. Frusciante, *Retired Circuit Court Judge, Florida Supreme Court Certified Circuit Civil & Family Mediator*

"You are about to make the most important decision of your life and that of an innocent child. So why not go in with all the knowledge you can? After reading this book, you will have all the tools to deal with most exciting times of your life."

—Judge David Young *(Ret.)*
Well-known former TV judge

"I litigated the Baby Emily case, which I believe inspired much legislative change to the adoption code, which remains a layered, complex statute. In your words, you provide common-sense discussion to lay persons on a subject most lawyers are challenged to understand."

—Steven M. Pesso, Esq., *Attorney in the seminal case of Baby Emily—this case changed the landscape of Florida adoption forever. Adoption of Baby E.A.W., 647 So.2d 918 (Fla. 4th DCA 1994)*

"This book is a great tool for those interested in pursuing adoption. It's easy to read and it sheds much-needed light on a complicated process."

—Elizabeth F. Schwartz, Esq.
Counselor at Law & Family Mediator
South Beach, Miami, Florida

"Useful information in a format suited for laymen. Very interesting, thought-provoking and informative."

—Joe and Cindy, *Adoptive Parents*
Jupiter, FL

"Entertaining and informative facts which every adoptive and prospective adoptive family should know. Also, fun to read!"

—Ked and Joanne, *Adoptive Parents*
Bluffton, IN

"Simplifies the otherwise complicated in every-day language. Enjoyed the read."

—Cathy and Keith, *Adoptive Parents*
Columbia, IL

"We found this book easy to understand and thought provoking. I would recommend that anyone planning to start thinking seriously about adoption read this book."

—Dana and Steve, *Adoptive Parents*
Raleigh, NC

"Placing my baby for adoption was one of the hardest but most rewarding things I've ever done. I would have liked to read this book before

I started the process, as it would have helped me understand what was going on behind the scenes."

—M. T., *Birth Mother*
  Virginia

LEGAL DISCLAIMER

Writing a book with facts on a subject like adoption is tricky business. Adoption is one of those fields which is left up to each state to regulate on its own. Aside from some interstate matters, such as the Interstate Compact on the Placement of Children, and federal matters, such as the Indian Child Welfare Act (both discussed in the pages to follow), adoption laws are pretty much handled on a state-by-state basis. Add to that the fact that Judges' decisions, referred to as "case law" (or *stare decisis* if you prefer Latin), plus frequent fluctuations in the legislation itself can and do have a significant effect on the process, and you've got an ever-changing, ever-evolving field!

The authors of this book are Florida-based attorneys, and have been helping people create their families through adoption as far back as 1973. Since January, 2000, approximately 60%

of the adoptions they assisted were performed for non-Florida families but 100% were completed under the very favorable Florida adoption law. Therefore it is advised that you use this book as a guide and tool, but not as the final word on adoption law in your state; even if you live in Florida. This information is offered to you by lawyers who are authors, not as *your* lawyers (that would cost you more than the cost of this book!). This book should help you be aware of some of the infinite number of issues that arise in adoption cases, so you can take that awareness with you through the process.

The facts, opinions, and asides herein are not legal treatises. There is room for debate over how any fact pattern might be interpreted or decided by any given court. Any lawyer well-versed in adoption might read any given paragraph and say something like, "True, but . . ." The smallest twist in a fact pattern can produce different results than those suggested here. Do not rely on this book for legal adoption advice!

This book is not an offer to do business. It's not an advertising tool or a solicitation of any kind. The authors are not your lawyers, nor are they seeking to be your lawyers. It will be fairly easy for you to find a lawyer in your area whose practice is focused on adoption. Google it, Bing it, Yahoo! it, or call your state's bar association for help in your area specific to your legal issue. You can also look for a local adoption support group for a referral. The resources are practically endless.

Further, you should also know that not every family lawyer is well-versed in adoption law and procedures. Not every lawyer professing to know about the broad field of "adoption" is aware of the issues relating to *your* type of adoption! Do the research, do your homework, and keep the information contained in this text in perspective.

As you navigate through the following pages, you will see that adoption can and almost always is a roller coaster ride. Numerous emotional, financial, social, moral, ethical, and other considerations come into play in the decision to start or expand a family through adoption. The one constant is that adoption is an extraordinarily risky adventure, emotionally and financially. Surrogacy is also discussed herein, and you'll see that it presents a different set of risks and rewards as compared to its cousin adoption.

One last point. You often hear in the world of real estate that the three most important considerations are: "LOCATION, LOCATION, LOCATION."[1] However, in choosing an adoption professional, we believe the three most important considerations are "EXPERIENCE, EXPERIENCE, EXPERIENCE!"

---

[1] William Thomas Dillard, The rules of business, (September 2, 1914 – February 8, 2002).

DEDICATION

This book is dedicated to all of the courageous women and men who have voluntarily chosen to undertake one of the most selfless acts, placing their child for adoption.

CONTENTS

CHAPTER 7

CHAPTER 8

FOREWORD

by Judge Harold Kahn

My wife Lisa and I adopted our two boys with the expert help of Robert and Jeffrey Kasky, the authors of this informative book on the nuts and bolts of the adoption process. Every day of the last twelve and a half years since our first child was placed for adoption with us at his birth, Lisa and I felt immense gratitude that adoption is legal and, when done properly, is in the best interests of all involved: the adopted children, the birth parents, the adoptive parents, and society as a whole. But adoption is not simple and must not be entered into lightly. There are numerous ways that a contemplated adoption can go awry, and often much heartache, as well as lost resources, that result when it does. As stated in this book, the adoption process is fraught with risks. For that reason, it is critical that all considering adoption know the basics of the adoption process that are spelled out in this book.

In addition to being an adoptive father, I am also a judge of a court that handles many adoptions each year. Although I have never been the adoption judge for my jurisdiction, I have filled-in for the adoption judge and, in that capacity, have presided over a number of adoption cases. Each one presents unique and special facts. The guiding consideration, as emphasized in this book, is the best interest of the child, taking into account the rights of the birth parents and prospective adoptive parents. All fifty states—and most of the rest of the world—quite properly require that a disinterested neutral judge approve a proposed adoption. This is because adoption implicates the concerns of our society at large, not just those involved in any particular adoption. By approving adoptions when done properly and disapproving them when not, judges carry out society's collective wisdom that adoption is beneficial, but only within carefully delineated boundaries designed to promote healthy and loving families.

As a parent of adopted children, I am a huge advocate of adoption, when done correctly (free of any taint of fraud, duress, and undue influence and in strict compliance with all applicable laws) and with sensitivity toward the needs of those involved. When done properly, an adoption is truly a win-win-win situation—a loving, nurturing home for a child who might not otherwise have one, a comforting alternative for birth parents not prepared or able to provide for the child, and the opportunity for the adoptive parents to experience the joy of parenthood.

The Kaskys' book provides extensive and much needed information about the basics of the adoption process for anyone considering adoption so that it can be done properly. This book identifies the many issues that need to be addressed by prospective birth parents and adoptive parents. But no book, no matter how long or detailed, is a substitute for receiving expert professional advice tailored to the particular circumstances and the needs of the those considering adoption. That is why, quite rightly, the book repeatedly reminds the reader that consultation with an adoption professional is a must. Unlike the preparation of taxes or the sale of a home, where it is possible—albeit risky—to do it yourself, an adoption must be guided by someone with demonstrated expertise about the rules of the adoption road.

Though the rules have changed considerably over time and vary from state to state, there is nothing new about adoption. An internet search discloses many websites discussing the history of adoption going back to the beginning of this country and as far back as ancient Rome and Greece. Likewise, there is abundant information about the happy and successful lives of adopted children. Recently many of us learned the adoption story of Steve Jobs, the genius behind Apple Inc. In his superb biography of Jobs, author Walter Isaacson quotes his subject on the impact that knowing he was adopted had on him. At page five of the book, Jobs is quoted: "There's some notion that because I was abandoned, I worked very hard so I could do well and make my [birth] parents wish they had me back, or some other such nonsense, but that's ridiculous . . . . Knowing that I was adopted may have made me feel more independent, but I have never felt abandoned. I've always felt special. They [his adoptive parents] were my parents 1,000%."[2] Other well-known adoptees include

---

[2] Isaacson, Walter. 2011. *Steve Jobs.* Simon & Schuster. First published 2011.

Presidents Bill Clinton and Gerald Ford, Jesse Jackson, Nat King Cole, and Marilyn Monroe. Famous adoptive parents include President Reagan, John McCain, Babe Ruth, and Willie Mays.

The long history of adoption and its widespread use underscores society's "adoption" of adoption as a tremendously important legal and ethical tool for the building and cohesion of the family, arguably the central institution of all of our lives. Thankfully, adoption is here to stay. But the success or failure of any particular contemplated adoption will depend in large measure on the knowledge and thoughtfulness of the persons involved. That is why a book like this is so critical. It provides a helpful introduction to many of the key concepts of the adoption process and enables the reader to have a better understanding of the possible pitfalls that may be encountered. I congratulate and thank the Kaskys for writing it.

Judge Harold Kahn
Father's Day (June 17) 2012

ABOUT THE 99 SERIES

The 99 Series is a collection of quick, easy-to-understand guides that spell it all out for you in the simplest format: 99 points, one lesson per page. The book series is the one-stop shop for all readers tired of looking all over for self-help books. The 99 Series brings it all to you under one umbrella! The bullet point format that is the basis for all the 99 Series books was created purposely for today's fast-paced society. Not only does information have to be at our finger tips . . . we need it quickly and accurately without having to do much research to find it. But don't be fooled by the easy-to-read format. Each of the books in the series contains very thorough discussions from our roster of professional authors so that all the information you need to know is compiled into one book!

We hope that you will enjoy this book as well as the rest of the series. If you've enjoyed our books, tell your friends. And if you feel we need to improve something, please feel free to give us your feedback at www.EmpireMediaWorldwide Inc.com.

Helen Georgaklis
Founder & CEO, EMWW, Inc.

ACKNOWLEDGMENTS

Jeff would like to thank:

Thank you first and foremost to my family: My putative father/law partner Robert Kasky, without whom I literally wouldn't be here; same goes for my mother Nancy; my sister Jill, who to this day still insists that she is an only child; my children Julian, Cameron & Holden Kasky, the coolest kids on Earth and the reason I do what I do every day; my awesome girlfriend Jeannette, for whom I could write 100 books, each filled with 99 things I love about her and Connor, and I'd only just be getting started.

Thank you to Margaret T. Snider, MSW, the one and only Executive Director One World Adoption Services has ever had, and a contributor to this book; to the Team Members at One World who have supported Marge's, my father's and my efforts to help people for all these years, including but not limited to Paula Ostroviesky, Estela Euceda, Jan Zuza, Alice Kasky, Leslie Levine, Maureen Bennett, Jessica Charbonneau, Jennifer Snyder, Juliana Triana, Suzanne Ludwig, Trina Augello, Cece, Tonya, and anyone I neglected to mention.

Thank you to all of the Judges and clerks who support our work by being there to do their part.

And last but certainly not least, thank you to all of the adoptive families who trusted us to help them create their families, and who've taken such good care of the kids we've entrusted to their care!

Robert would like to thank:

I, too, have many people to thank and because Jeff and I are both father and son and partners in this emotionally rewarding profession, the people to whom I owe thanks are the same as Jeff's. I would also like to add to Jeff's list thanks to my grandchildren Jack and Jamie, who inspire me every day.

INTRODUCTION

Before we begin the 99 list, a story for you from Jeff:

I graduated from Nova Southeastern University Shepard Broad Law Center in 1995. Unlike many of my peers, I did not go straight from college to law school, but did a stint in the music business at The William Morris Agency in between.

Post music business, I thought that my baby-sitting days were over, and that handling adoptions as a lawyer would be relatively mundane, safe, and emotionally rewarding but otherwise uninteresting. BOY WAS I WRONG!

One of the many great things about the field of adoption—when you're actually on the front lines, working with the people and not hiding behind a desk—is that every time you have the nerve to say something like "Well now I've seen it all!" you find you haven't seen the least of it. Also, you don't have to use hypotheticals when describing possibilities. If you've done this long enough, there's a true story for every freakish consideration. You can't make this stuff up and fortunately you don't even have to. Here is one of them:

I was awakened late one night by a crying female voice on the other end of the phone. Nan (not her real name of course) advised me that she was three months pregnant, didn't want to have another abortion, and wasn't able at this time in her life to provide for the baby in the best way possible. She advised that she was 35, a local entertainer, and that she knew who the father was, and that although he didn't know of her plan to place the baby, he would be cooperative.

Upon my inquiry, Nancy told me that the father of the pregnancy was a 17-year-old guy named Warren (not his real name of course), and that he was a 6'5" tall, 350 lb. Elvis impersonator. What did you say?!?! If it were a movie you'd have heard the needle go across the record. I seriously thought she was joking. I wanted to question Nan's sanity at that point, but she sounded so matter-of-fact about it that I was leaning towards believing her story.

I asked Nan how I might be able to reach this very interesting sounding teen. She told me that his cell phone had been turned off, but that there is a nightclub in the area which hosts an Elvis karaoke night on the 1st Tuesday of every month, and that he never misses it. Wouldn't chya know that the 1st Tuesday of the month was the very next day?

I paid my $5 and walked in. The bar was a little like the Mos Eisley scene in Star Wars—there was a little bit of everything, and it wasn't all necessarily from this planet. The one thing they all had in common, though, were that they were Elvises. There were short Elvises, tall Elvises, big Elvises, small Elvises. There were Asian Elvises, black Elvises, sane Elvises and quack Elvises. There were Elvises from his young, handsome days, and Elvises from his fat, sloppy days. The one thing all of these Elvises had in common was that they were there in tribute to The King, and I respected their dedication.

The music was in full effect, and the Elvises were enjoying each other's performance. I watched an Asian Elvis do a duet with a white Elvis, trading lines on "Blue Suede Shoes." Raucous and awesome. And loud.

It wasn't hard to find Warren, as he was by far the youngest, tallest and fattest Elvis in the bar. Warren was wearing a very large version of the white spandex jumpsuit with all of the sparkly trimmings, and an identically trimmed white cape. He had the sideburns, the big glasses and on top of the costume he actually had a fairly Elvisy-looking face. I was impressed.

I approached Warren and put out my hand to shake his. He had to bend to hear me, with him being so tall and the music so loud. I asked him if I could speak with him for a moment, and we made our way back out through the crowd.

Once outside, I introduced myself to Warren and explained to him that I was there to discuss the adoption and to make sure he would consent or at least not contest. His shoulders dropped a bit and I had the feeling that this is the first time that the realities of life had hit this 17-year-old performer. Warren told me that he had a feeling he'd be hearing from someone regarding this situation, and that he agreed that neither of them was in any position to try to raise the baby when it came, and that he would sign the adoption papers.

One of the things I like to do in my practice is actually carefully go over paperwork, even if whomever it is just wants to 'sign and get it over with.' It wasn't the right time and/or place to sit down and review documents, so I advised Warren of his right to have his own attorney in this matter, left the paperwork with him, and arranged to meet him two days later for lunch at the IHOP down the street.

Leaving the karaoke bar after midnight, I called my father and asked "so this is what I went to law school for?"

On Thursday I left my office at around 11 am to travel the 45 minutes or so that it would take to get to the IHOP. I was in the middle of a call when I left, had already done a hundred things that morning, and had a thousand left. I was on the phone the whole way to the meeting, on the phone stepping out of the car into the parking lot, and still on the phone as I was seated alone in a booth in this busy lunchtime IHOP, back to the door, waiting for my guest to arrive. In short, I was not focused on meeting with Warren, and that's why I was so shocked when suddenly, standing before me was Warren, in a jumpsuit, cape, pompadour, sideburns, glasses—full Elvis gear.

So as it turns out, a lot of people live their lives as Elvis. Not just for First Tuesday Night of the Month Karaoke, but for real. Warren, at 17 tender years, had taken on the persona of Elvis Presley in his permanent daily life.

For several reasons, and needless to say, people stared and pointed. The brave ones approached. Warren was more than happy to pose for pictures and sign autographs, and fortunately he also signed the papers I needed him to sign. Yes, I checked his ID and yes, of course, he was Elvis (sans glasses) in his Florida driver license picture.

I never saw Warren again after that day, but I've seen many pictures of the baby boy that Nan delivered and placed for adoption, and he's getting tall!

You may find some of our stories enlightening, sad or even funny. There are a thousand more where these came from, and they're all true!

Please consider joining our Facebook page. Search the title, 99 things you wish you knew before…Choosing adoption and 'like' the page. We will be taking questions and comments, posting bonus content and stories, and letting you know if we're coming to speak at an event near you!

We are available for speaking engagements and can be contacted via our Manager, Paula Ostroviesky, via e-mail to info@OneWorldAdoption.com.

CHAPTER 1

GENERAL FACTS ABOUT ADOPTION

#1: A Single Person vs. Married Person

A single person has the same rights to adopt a child as does a married couple.

This is not to say that it's as easy for a single parent to adopt as it is for a couple to adopt. There are a variety of factors involved, not the least of which is the birth parents' preferences for a couple versus single-parent adoptive family, if that is the case. It is not uncommon for a birth mother who was raised by a single parent to prefer a married couple.

#2: "Homosexual" Prohibition Abolished in Florida

Until 2011, Florida was the only state in the U.S. with an outright prohibition on adoption by "a homosexual." That was changed recently by a line of appellate court rulings.

Any person who is otherwise qualified to adopt can adopt a child whether or not he/she is "a homosexual." The Florida legislature did not remove the prohibition, but the courts did. This, like everything, is subject to change by legislative decision or higher court action.

Jeff Kasky's very basic analysis of the constitutionality of prohibition against "a homosexual" from adopting, go to http://www.sfgn.com and type 'Kasky' into the search box (mid-page, right column). The article is called "The Legislature Can't Write."

#3: It's Easier to Get an Abortion than Place for Adoption

In most jurisdictions it is infinitely easier to get an abortion than to place a baby for adoption.

Birth mother consent, birth father consent, Native American Indian Tribe consent . . . these things are not needed to terminate a pregnancy but are generally needed to complete an adoption. Adoption necessitates the consideration of the rights of many different individuals and entities in order to legally complete the process. The process is not easy legally or emotionally for all parties involved and for this reason as well as so many others birth parents should be commended for making the decision to place a baby for adoption. It's definitely not the easy way out!

#4: Some States Have "Open Adoption"

Some states have "open adoption" laws promoting agreed-upon contact and communication after the adoption is finalized and some state laws are totally silent on this subject thus rendering any such agreement a moral, but not legal, obligation.

The degree of openness, if any, in an adoption is by agreement between the birth parents and the prospective adoptive parents. This can include anything from periodic pictures and e-mails to videos, phone calls, visits, attendance at important functions and more.

When considering the degree of openness to which a birth parent or adoptive parent is comfortable, remember to keep the child's best interests in mind. Just because you want or will agree to a certain degree of openness doesn't mean that that degree of openness is what's best for the child's emotional and psychological development.

#5: Adoption Facilitators are Illegal in Some Jurisdictions

Make sure that your adoption professional is working legally within your jurisdiction. The easiest way to do this is to either contact an attorney whose practice is focused on adoption or call your state's adoption licensing authority (i.e., Department of Children & Families). Nothing beats a personal recommendation from someone you know who used a professional's services successfully.

#6: Must You Become a Parent?

There is no constitutional right to be a parent, and there is no law that says you have to be a parent.

Adoption professionals try, on a daily basis, to find the best possible home for every child, born or as-yet unborn, entrusted to them. That may or may not be you. However, there is nothing in the Constitution of the United States of America or any state's constitution stating that every couple or adult has the right to be a parent.

By contrast, it is our professional opinion that every child has a right to receive the best possible upbringing for their specific circumstance. One of the most challenging and rewarding facets of our jobs as adoption professionals is to try to match each child—born or as-yet unborn—with the family that can best raise him or her.

Likewise, there is social and familial pressure after marriage to be a parent. Everyone wants to know, "So when is the baby coming? When are you going to make me a grandparent?" etc. Whether or not to become a parent is a personal decision to be made by you, not by pressure from friends or family! If you have been unable to conceive and are seeking alternatives to pregnancy the usual way, make very sure that you even want to be a parent before you adopt a baby. You may find that your life is full and more enjoyable without kids!

#7: Your Adoption Professional Should Be Available 24/7

Your adoption professional or a designee should be available 24/7 for phone calls from birth parents. Ask your adoption professional how he/she handles after-hours or weekend communications with birth parents. Adoptions are definitely not a 9 to 5, Monday through Friday, experience. Birth Parents will often have emergencies which can't wait until the next business morning. These emergencies include, of course, labor and delivery! If your adoption professional goes on voice mail after hours and weekends, you may wish to get a toll-free number so that the birth parents can contact you directly if the adoption professional is unreachable.

> ***Case in point:*** *In a case we worked on, Patty called our Agency at 2:55 a.m. Robert was on call that night and answered, spending about a half-hour discussing Patty's dilemma with her. She was due in two weeks and had been living in denial of the pregnancy for 8 ½ months!*

Immediate action was necessary to give Patty and the unborn child the services Patty was requesting.

Robert explained the adoption program to Patty and set up a meeting for the very same afternoon. The pre-delivery paperwork was complete and filed with the court. It's a good thing she called when she did, because Patty delivered only a week later, and placed the baby for adoption with the family with whom she was matched through the Agency.

After the dust settled, we asked Patty why she called at 2:55 a.m. She told us that the day before that call, she had tried to contact five agencies or attorneys. Three were out-of-state entities and not licensed to provide services in Florida, one social worker chastised her for both waiting so long to do something about the pregnancy, and for having her second baby out of wedlock, and one number was out of business. Patty had thought that she would just leave a message at our office and hope to receive a call the next day, and was shocked to actually get a live lawyer on the phone at that ungodly hour! She was surprised and impressed with our commitment to 24 hours a day/7 days a week service which we not only advertise but actually deliver.

So, a family was created that day. The Agency has never used voice mail and likely never will.

#8: Must Have a Home Study

With limited exceptions, every family seeking to adopt a child must have a comprehensive home study performed by a state-licensed social worker and it must describe the family, its expected ability to parent a child and, among others, contain a description of the family's education, health, legal, criminal, social and financial background.

When we are reviewing a family's home study, in addition to the above we like to see a statement regarding any drinking or smoking habits of the prospective adoptive family, and hobbies, interests, and anything that makes them special or different. These are items that can distinguish your family from others, and may be the difference in any given situation as to whether you are matched with a birth mother.

Placement of a child with a family without a home study may violate local, state and federal laws and compacts, depending on the facts of the case.

Exceptions for the Home Study requirement include adoptive parents with a close biological relation to the child to be adopted, and step-parent adoptions.

It is crucial that you know beyond the shadow of any doubt whether a home study is needed for your adoption. If you attempt to undertake an adoption and you do it without a home study in a case wherein a home study is legally required, a host of problems can follow. Consult an experienced professional in your area.

#9: Anyone Can Be Adopted, Not Just Babies!

If a woman finds that after a period of time—a week, a month, three months, a year, or even longer—she cannot provide for the child as well as she would like the child to be provided for, she can place the child for adoption.

Further, laws will vary, but typically the placement of an older child will trigger a revocation period during which the birth parents can revoke their consent to the adoption and regain custody of the child.

In Florida, if a child is over 6 months of age when placed for adoption, the birth parents have the right to revoke their consent within 3 business days of signing the consent. There is no need to show fraud or duress—just a change of mind in sufficient.

> ***Case in point:*** *In a recent Florida case, a multi-millionaire on trial for DUI manslaughter actually adopted his adult girlfriend, creating inheritance rights in her which may have the effect of protecting tens or hundreds of millions of dollars of his wealth from the pending civil suit in the matter. The civil suit ended up settling for 40 million dollars, the rich guy was found guilty and is appealing the finding, and his girlfriend is now his daughter. That adoption is legal, although solid arguments have been made that it violates the spirit and the legislative intent of the adoption statutes.*

CHAPTER 2

RISKS OF ADOPTION AND RIGHTS & RESPONSIBILITIES

#10: Adoption Is Risky

Adoptions are extremely risky legally, emotionally and financially. Even when everything is done by the book, adoptions can result in financial and emotional disaster. There is no fool-proof law or method to conducting a private adoption. Undertaking the process is a huge leap of faith; thus, to minimize, but not eliminate, the risks, prospective adoptive parents should seriously consider using an experienced professional to whom they are personally referred.

The general risks of adoption are plentiful. Here are just a few of them:

- The birth parents may never have intended to place the unborn baby for adoption and may simply be seeking money for living expenses or other uses during the pregnancy.
- The birth parents may be working with and receiving funds from multiple adoption professionals in one or more states.
- The background information provided by the birth parents may be intentionally or inadvertently materially incorrect insofar as medical and other facts are concerned.
- The birth mother may incorrectly identify someone as the birth father and may also provide intentionally or unintentionally misleading information about him and his whereabouts.
- The ethnicity, medical status, and many other important factors may be inaccurately reported.
- The birth mother may state that the birth father is not supporting her and that he has abandoned her when, in fact, he has done quite the opposite thus creating a potential legal obstacle to successfully completing the adoption.

- Regardless of the insistence of and assistance from the adoption professional, the birth mother may not exercise healthy habits during the pregnancy (i.e., smoking, drug use, and/or drinking alcohol).
- The birth mother could have a miscarriage or a stillbirth.
- The child could have unforeseen physical, medical, or developmental issues.
- The birth parents can change their minds and keep the baby with no consequences to them

#11: A Birth Mother Has the Right to Privacy

A birth mother has the right of privacy and may place a baby for adoption without identifying the child's biological father. She also has the right not to have her name known by the prospective adoptive family. Birth parents ought to provide accurate, factual and not misleading information to the adoptive family throughout the adoption process.

#12: Consent Given Based On Fraud or Under Duress

A birth parent's consent to an adoption may be withdrawn if it was obtained by fraud or duress.

Fraud: If consent is obtained based on fraud, it is not really consent and can be withdrawn. Consent must be given fair and square. Examples of fraud include willful misrepresentation of key information regarding the adoptive family; promises of pictures or future contact when the prospective adoptive family never really intended to do so; and an unfulfilled promise to provide the birth mother with financial and/or emotional support, as permitted by law, after the birth of the child.

For example, if a birth mother requires that her baby be placed with a Catholic family only, and a family is presented to her as Catholic when they are known by themselves and the adoption entity to be not Catholic, this is fraud, and the birth mother may be permitted to revoke her consent to the adoption and therefore take her baby back.

Under Florida law, a birth mother is able to receive reasonable and necessary maintenance and support (living expenses) during her pregnancy and for up to six weeks thereafter. The law does not require such assistance, but the assistance is legally available when needed.

Case in point: *The prospective adoptive family, through its attorney, promises to provide Suzie with the legally-permissible six week post-partum financial assistance which she will need to help her get back on her feet after her Caesarean section. At the time the promise is made, the family is well aware that they are running very low on funds and that they will not be able to provide the promised support. However, they feel that if they don't promise her the money, she will back out of the adoption.*

The baby is born, the consent is signed by Suzie, and the family refuses to provide the six weeks post-partum support.

Is this fraud? Does Suzie have any recourse to invalidate or withdraw her consent? Should she even do that if she can?

As with many legal questions there are no certain answers. The tiniest difference in the facts surrounding the controversy can produce dramatically different results from one case to another. Even the same set of facts can produce different results when heard by two different tiers of fact, be they judge or jury.

The takeaway here is that you don't ever want to find yourself in the midst of a controversy or disagreement with a baby's future at stake in the outcome. Don't make promises that you don't intend to keep! Make sure that everything you've promised or that has been promised to you is written unambiguously and put into an Agreement.

There is also a moral question at hand: Even if Suzie would be able to revoke her consent legally, does that make it the right thing to do? There is no answer to this question, but it's something to think about and discuss with your adoption professional.

> ***Case in point:*** *Abbie is a devout born again Christian. Although she is tolerant and understanding of the beliefs of others, Abbie adamantly insists that the baby she's placing for adoption be adopted by a church-going born again Christian family.*
>
> *The adoption entity presents a wonderful family to Abbie, but the family is Catholic. In preparation of a meeting with Abbie, the entity advises the family to say they're born again Christians if asked, because Abbie would want them to be. They do as they're told.*

Two weeks after the birth, while perusing the announcement section of the local paper, Abbie sees that the family who adopted her baby is having a baptism at Our Lady of Lourdes Catholic Church. Obviously they are most certainly not born again Christians.

Fraud or not fraud? We think it is, and as such Abbie would succeed in an effort to revoke her consent, which was never freely given to this family. However, is that her only recourse? Is that the best way to handle this case?

Duress: Consent to adoption must be given fair and square. If consent is given based on threats of arrest or other similar coercive action, the consent is not freely given and therefore may be withdrawn.

Generalized social and financial pressures which lead a birth parent to make an adoption decision for their child are not the types of pressures which would trigger the right to withdraw an otherwise fairly-given consent. Indeed, it is usually exactly those pressures which typically lead to the adoption decision in the first place, and giving birth parents the right to revoke based on those elements would collapse the entire adoption system.

Case in point: A young woman named Cassidy contacted us during her pregnancy for help with her adoption plan. Cassidy had been physically and emotionally abused by the father of the pregnancy and needed our help in finding safe housing, money for groceries, and the other day-to-day expenses of living. We made all of the arrangements and Cassidy—at her request—met and spent a lot of quality time with the prospective adoptive couple, Allen and Barbara.

When the big day came, Allen and Barbara were in the hospital with Cassidy, as she requested. Barbara was pulled into the delivery room and witnessed the birth of her baby girl. Things couldn't have been better! Cassidy signed the adoption consent and related paperwork at the prescribed time, and the baby went home with the family. Cassidy received several post-partum counseling sessions.

Cut to three months later. We receive a letter from a lawyer along with a Petition to Revoke/ Invalidate Consent and Return Child to Parents. Wouldn't you know that Cassidy and Prince Charming got back together? They decided that Cassidy gave her consent under duress, the duress being that she was scared that she wouldn't be able to take care of the baby by herself. Now that she and the biological father were back together, she wanted the baby back so they could raise him together.

The ruling: NO! This is not the type of duress contemplated by the statute. Cassidy gave her consent freely and voluntarily, without being "forced" to do so by anyone. That litigation cost Allen and Barbara thousands of dollars and untold sleepless days and nights, but the outcome was correct.

Case in point: *Jessica is pregnant and on probation. She delivers the baby, who tests positive for cocaine, and announces soon after delivery that she does not intend to place the baby for adoption, but to keep it and parent instead. Upon learning of this decision, the lawyer for the family who was supposed to have adopted the baby advises Jessica that if she doesn't sign the adoption consent then her probation officer would get a call regarding the positive drug test. Jessica doesn't want to go back to jail, so she grudgingly signs the consent.*

Several months later, with her legal matters all cleared up, Jessica makes a motion in court to invalidate her consent based on the notion that it was obtained through duress, and was therefore never consent in the first place.

In the scenario described above, Jessica wins. Her consent was obtained through duress and was therefore not given freely and voluntarily.

#13: Birth Parent May Place Before Termination of Parental Rights (TPR)

"TPR" stands for termination of parental rights. This can be done voluntarily, as in adoption, or involuntarily, as in removal of a child from the parent by the State.

If a state agency has removed a child from a birth parent, and is moving towards terminating that parent's parental rights but the TPR has not yet been ordered by a court of law, the parent may place the child for private adoption and have rights not otherwise available if their parental rights were terminated by the State. This provision enables a birth parent to place a child with a permanent adoptive family and avoid the child being placed in foster care. The family must of course be an appropriate adoptive family and have a valid home study.

Under the newly-passed Florida statute, the Court (meaning the Judge) is required to advise every person whose parental rights may be terminated against their will that they have the right to do a private adoption through a private, licensed adoption agency, as opposed to involuntarily through the state's embattled public service program.

> **Case in point:** *Parental rights are transferable, and are retained until voluntarily or involuntarily terminated by a court of competent jurisdiction.*
>
> *A couple of years ago, Reba, a woman whom we worked with chose at the end to keep the baby which she had been planning to place for adoption. Reba's lifestyle, however, was legally incompatible with raising a child in the State of Florida. Specifically, she had a pain pill habit that caused her to prostitute for money for pills. The Department of Children & Families received a tip about Reba's behavior, and took custody of the newborn whom she had originally been planning to place for adoption. They removed her five-year-old, too.*
>
> *Reba called us distraught and told us the situation, and that DCF had told her that*

they were likely going to attempt to seek involuntary termination of her parental rights to the kids. She told us that she realized that she had made an emotional knee-jerk mistake by keeping the newborn, and that the stress of trying to raise the baby created this whole problem. Reba advised us that she wanted the family who was supposed to have adopted the baby to adopt both kids so that DCF wouldn't leave them in foster care for an extended period, and wouldn't eventually place them for adoption with unknown, and possibly separate, families.

Because Reba's parental rights had not yet been legally terminated, she still held them, despite the fact that DCF had actual custody of the two kids. Reba and her boyfriend signed the Consent and the related documents and thus transferred legal rights to the children to this Agency. The next hurdle was the actual legal intervention into the DCF case.

One would think that the State would be glad that a private agency, licensed by the State itself, was willing to take a case out of the overworked, overburdened, and underfinanced system, but one would be surprised. DCF, generally speaking and for reasons we consider inexplicable, sometimes chooses to put up a fight against its own licensees. It happens more than it should.

Ultimately, however, the Judge in the case understood the law and made the right decision. The children were turned over to the custody of our office and immediately placed in the pre-adoptive home. After the statutorily-required period of time and supervision, the adoption was completed in favor of the family who had been devastated a few months prior!

That was two years ago. As of this writing, both kids are doing very well in their permanent family, and Reba still requests and receives periodic pictures and updates.

#14: Biological Father May Not Have Legal Rights

Laws vary from state-to-state, but a man who is not married to the birth mother may not automatically have legal rights to a child, even if it is proven that he is the biological father of the child! Some states require the birth father to take affirmative actions to preserve and protect any parental rights he may have, and provide a deadline after which it is too late for him to assert parental rights.

Furthermore, some states require that if an unmarried putative biological father wishes to assert his parental rights, if any, he must agree to and pay for a DNA test to establish whether he is even the biological father before he can even attempt to assert rights.

#15: Affidavit of Non-Paternity

A birth father may surrender any rights he has to a child before the birth of the child. Some states allow for the biological father of an unborn child to sign a document—in Florida it's called an Affidavit of Non-Paternity—effectively waiving the need for him to consent to the adoption. This can be accomplished before the birth of the baby.

Florida law no longer requires that the putative father even admit that he might be the biological father. He, too, has the right of privacy, and can simply agree not to pursue any rights that he may have without admitting or denying that he may have planted the proverbial seed.

Most states require some type of contribution from the birth father to the well-being of the baby, even during the pregnancy. The support must be reasonable and regular, as opposed to meaningless and sporadic. A $20 bill three or four times during the pregnancy probably isn't going to cut it. The birth father's ability to provide support will be taken into account, but the big picture question, which the court must answer, is whether the efforts made were done with meaning and purpose, and not just window dressing.

#16: Incarcerated Parent Might Not Be Required to Consent

In Florida and some other states, a birth father who is incarcerated for a significant portion of a child's minority is not required to consent to an adoption based on his "abandonment" of the child.

A birth father cannot stop an adoption if he's going to be incarcerated for a significant portion of the child's minority, as determined by the presiding Judge and based on the child's age and the child's need for a permanent and stable home. Oftentimes it is not exactly clear how much longer an individual is going to be incarcerated, considering such factors as parole, probation, gain time, prison overcrowding, etc. This can be an area of contentious debate if it arises in a case and the final decision is made by the Judge.

#17: Certain Crimes Preclude the Father from Asserting Rights

There are certain crimes which preclude the birth father from asserting any parental rights. For example, many states will not allow a birth father to assert parental rights if the pregnancy was the result of the sexual assault of the birth mother by the birth father. Child abuse-related crimes, sex crimes, and violent felonies are other matters that are probably dispositive as to whether a person's consent can be waived.

#18: Diligent Search, Marriage to Birth Mother

Whether or not a birth father is married to a birth mother can make all the difference in what, if any, rights he has to the child. A man who is married to the mother of a child—whether it is his biological child or not—is deemed to be the legal father of the child and has far fewer tasks to undertake to protect his rights if he contests an adoption plan. As the legal father, his consent to an adoption is required or can be waived if he cannot be located after a diligent search and other appropriate efforts are made to notify him of the proposed termination of his parental rights and subsequent adoption of the child.

If a birth father's identity is known but his whereabouts are not, a "diligent search" of numerous sources must be made to locate him. Efforts to find him in various real estate records, hospitals, phone books, criminal justice systems, utility companies, etc. must be made in strict compliance with applicable state law.

If a diligent search is successful in locating a birth father, he must either be served with a summons requiring his presence in court at a hearing or efforts must be made to provide him with personal service of process. If those efforts do not result in the birth father being personally served, service can be accomplished, as noted below, by publication.

If a diligent search is unsuccessful in locating a birth father, a notice must be published in a local qualified media notifying the birth father that a hearing to terminate his parental rights has been set on a date certain before a named Judge. His failure to personally appear may result in his parental rights being terminated by default.

That said, however, a Judge has the discretion to reschedule the hearing to give the father yet another opportunity to appear in court or to terminate his parental rights based on his non-appearance in court.

> ***Case in point:*** *A woman came to us and advised us that she was pregnant and wanted to place the baby for adoption due to her present inability to provide for the child. She advised that she thought that she was married but was unsure. She said that she hadn't seen the man to whom she may be married in over ten years. An investigation revealed that she had legally married a man about 11 years prior, and that the husband has been incarcerated in federal prison in Arizona for the past 5+ years. As the legal father, his consent was required. Luckily he gave us no trouble whatsoever. We sent the Consent to the prison and it was executed correctly and immediately, and the adoption went through without a hitch.*

Side note: If he was not found by diligent search, he could have been served his constitutionally-required Notice by publishing a legal notice to him once-a-week for four consecutive weeks notifying him that his parental rights were the subject of a termination action.

CHAPTER 3

BIRTH PARENT EXPENSES

#19: Some states Allow Assistance with Expenses

Some states permit licensed adoption professionals to assist a birth mother in the payment of her reasonable and necessary living expenses during the pregnancy and for a period of time after delivery and placement of the child for adoption, and some states disallow financial assistance of any kind in connection with adoption.

The laws are different across the country, and sometimes those laws are even interpreted differently from county-to-county within a state, but many jurisdictions allow for the birth mother's reasonable expenses to be covered during the pregnancy. However, BE CAREFUL! In some states it's a crime to provide the birth mother with any type of financial support.

The competing theories are based on the notions of not wanting to let people "sell" their babies by receiving a benefit of any kind whatsoever for placing them for adoption, versus wanting to provide the birth mother with at least the basic living requirements so at least she has the funds to be healthy and nourished during the pregnancy. The government has an interest in making sure that babies are born as healthy as possible—it costs the government a lot of money to take care of a baby born with disease or malnutrition.

#20: Court May Be Required to Approve Expenses

In states where prenatal financial support to the birth mother is allowed, a court may be required to pre-approve a list of all costs and expenses anticipated to be paid by a family adopting a child when those expenses exceed a certain level.

Your adoption professional should be able to explain to you and to the court with jurisdiction over your case, with a fair degree of specificity, what the costs are of taking care of the birth mother's reasonable living expenses during her pregnancy, where allowed. That said, unexpected costs are the norm, so it's reasonable for your professional to provide you with an "estimated" projection of costs and expenses.

#21: Expenses Assistance

Florida permits licensed adoption professionals to assist birth mothers in the payment of their reasonable and necessary living expenses throughout the pregnancy and for a period of up to six weeks after delivery of the child placed for adoption. All of such expenditures must be reported to and approved by the appropriate court. The approval step usually takes place at or around the time of the final hearing.

This is not an invitation for a financial windfall for the birth mother, or an opportunity for the adoptive parents' bank account to be drained. This must be done carefully and with permission from the court, and the expenses must be reasonable and necessary. The post-delivery support is designed to let a birth mother heal physically and emotionally for a reasonable period of time before she has to jump out of bed and go back to work or school. If the support is not necessary, i.e., if her parents are supporting her or if her significant other pays the bills, it's not allowed.

#22: Expenses Assistance Not Available for the Birth Father

Although reasonable and necessary living expenses may be advanced for a birth mother, no such expenses may be paid on behalf of a birth father.

The support expenses in an adoption are allowed by law so that the baby's health will not be compromised by factors relating to finances. If the birth mother doesn't have the funds to maintain a healthy diet, can't get appropriate care, doesn't have a safe and comfortable residence, etc., the baby will have less of a probability of being born without health-related concerns. The birth father is not pregnant, and thus does not qualify for the financial support allowed to the birth mother.

Case in point: *A birth couple whom we helped included the unemployed boyfriend of the birth mother, along with his child from a previous relationship. When apprising the Judge of the facts of the case and requesting permission to provide financial support for the birth mother, the Judge adamantly refused to allow us to provide the full rent and utility bill, ruling that the boyfriend was not pregnant and could work to provide for himself and his son.*

The Judge decided that Florida law does not allow the prospective adoptive family to provide financial support for a person who is not pregnant and planning to place a baby for adoption. We agree with this Judge's reading and interpretation of the law, but the implementation was not so simple. Do we divide the rent into three, accounting for the birth father's young son? How about the utility bills and other expenses?

Ultimately the birth father and his child were kicked out of the apartment by the birth mother after a fight, and the prospective adoptive family ended up having to absorb the entire amount of rent, utilities, etc. anyway.

Case in point: *We were working with a woman named Janet on her second adoption plan with our Agency when Janet was convicted of trafficking in narcotics and sentenced to three years in state prison. Janet had been living in reasonably comfortable style, having had all of her basic living expenses covered by the adoptive family, though the Agency, for the several months leading up to her incarceration.*

Janet expected that her rent and grocery money would continue, as her husband, Bill, and their three children were still living in the residence where Janet lived before she was sent away.

Florida law only allows for the reasonable and necessary bills of the birth mother. Payment of living expenses for the birth mother's family is not contemplated or permitted. Therefore, aside from some prison commissary money which we sent for snacks and items of personal hygiene, we discontinued sending rent and gift cards for groceries.

Janet and Bill were furious, demanding to know how they were expected to support their family without our help. The prospect of turning off the X-Box, getting off the couch, and getting a job was the furthest thing from Bill's reality. The applicable adoption laws were not written to give handouts to lazy people. They were written to support the health of a woman who is pregnant, so that the baby would have a better shot at receiving the appropriate nutrition in the womb.

Janet eventually went into labor in the exercise yard at the prison. She was shackled, as is the custom, and driven to the hospital in a prison van. One of her wrists was handcuffed to the hospital bed as she delivered a healthy baby girl in the presence of hospital medical staff and an armed guard. Two days later, in the presence of a Notary Public, two witnesses, a court reporter, an armed guard, and Robert, Janet signed the Consent to Adoption, still handcuffed to her hospital bed.

The baby was adopted by a wonderful adoptive mother and they are doing fine! Janet has been requesting and receiving pictures. We have not heard from Bill.

#23: Counseling Should Be Available

Provisions should be made to incur expenses for counseling services to be made available to the birth parents, if requested, both before birth and on a post-delivery basis. The availability and use of such professional services may serve as a valuable tool in helping to assure that the birth parents receive input concerning the whole emotional adoption process as well as what can be expected afterwards from an independent source. It is not unusual for an adoption agency to have a fully qualified counselor on staff (i.e., an employee with a Master's Degree in Social Work) to offer counseling services on a spontaneous basis and many times without the need to have an appointment.

#24: Avoid Providing Actual Cash

If you are planning to adopt an as-yet unborn child, and are matched with a birth mother, you and/or your legal designee (agency or lawyer) should try to avoid providing actual cash support whenever possible.

When supporting a birth mother financially, consider sending gift cards (e.g., grocery, Walmart, etc.) instead of cash or checks for her reasonable and necessary living expenses. Some people are less responsible with cash, and often there are fees involved in the cashing of checks. A gift card will not guarantee that the money is used for the purposes intended, but it will offer more of a likelihood than cash, and is at least somewhat traceable and may be cancelled if stolen or lost.

#25: Reasonable and Necessary Maintenance and Support

Typically, reasonable and necessary living expenses of a birth mother can be paid through an agency or an attorney and can cover the period of the pregnancy and sometimes a period afterwards to give the birth mother time to reorganize and regroup and resume her former life.

Although each adoption has its own characteristics and nuances, the expenses which are generally considered reasonable and necessary include rent (and sometimes a security deposit to the landlord), utilities (paid to the provider of the services), food (amount will vary if the birth mother has children living with her), transportation (to get to the doctor, hospital, lab, and other necessary appointments only), and things like maternity clothing, prescriptions not covered by a medical plan, and personal hygiene products. It is the responsibility of the agency or attorney to disburse these funds and then to report such expenditures to the court at some time during the adoption process.

#26: Don't Get Scammed!

There are endless versions of similar adoption scams that go around and around and will never stop. If persons unknown to you but holding themselves out as a prospective birth parent asks you to send them money, no matter how much or little, don't do it! Not only might you run afoul of your state's laws regarding how and whether you can provide financial support for a birth mother, but you are more likely than not being scammed!

> ***Case in point:*** *We get this call at least twice a year. A woman calls pretending to be a nurse or social worker at a hospital. In fact, the call comes through on caller ID listing the hospital's main telephone number. The "nurse" claims that there's a woman who delivered a healthy baby a day or two prior, and she's being discharged first thing tomorrow morning. She doesn't want to*

parent the baby, and wants us to place the baby for adoption for her.

The "nurse" has decided to call an agency several hours away because the birth mother is afraid of running into the birth father, who was physically abusive to her (as if the birth father is sitting in the lobby of every closer adoption agency).

The "nurse" wants to put the birth mother and the baby on a bus and have her delivered right around the corner from our office— how convenient! All I have to do is Western Union $300 to the "nurse" to cover the $75 bus ticket, plus some clothes and food and spending money for the birth mother while she's on her three hour trip.

I'm not going to fall for that, but would a desperate prospective adoptive family? These scammers are more likely to target families directly, through their internet ads or in states where prospective adoptive families are allowed to place their own print ads seeking a baby.

This is not the only scam, there are plenty of others. Don't fall for them.

#27: Adoption Myth

If a woman accepts financial assistance during her pregnancy from an adoption agency or prospective adoptive parents, she is selling her baby. FALSE!

There are many who feel that even though certain types of financial assistance are legal, you are a bad person for accepting any money of any kind whatsoever if you are placing a baby for adoption.

The theory for allowing certain expenses to be paid is based on the public policy that we, as a society, would rather these children be born having come from a reasonably healthy pregnancy. Therefore, expenses that cover basic living needs can be provided, as described elsewhere in this text.

There are a handful of states that expressly prohibit certain types of financial assistance to the birth mother (as of this writing, these states are Illinois, Kentucky, Minnesota, Montana, New Hampshire, North Dakota, and Wisconsin). The rest of the states have varying degrees of allowance of payment of these expenses, subject to legislative change.

We believe that there is nothing wrong with accepting reasonable and legal financial assistance during the pregnancy if the ultimate effect is to help the birth mother and the unborn child remain healthy and get a healthy, clean start to life!

CHAPTER 4

INTERSTATE AND NATIVE AMERICAN-INDIAN ADOPTIONS

#28: ICPC

The Interstate Compact on the Placement of Children (ICPC) is a procedural state law in every state and it is designed to protect the interests of the children who are being adopted as well as to protect the integrity of the state laws of both the state where the child is born and where he/she will be residing during and after the adoption process.

So, even if you do not live in the state where the baby was born, you are permitted to adopt the baby if you comply with ICPC.

#29: You Need Professional Help in Navigating ICPC

The technical requirements of the ICPC process make it difficult to successfully navigate without the help of an experienced professional. Traveling interstate with an adopted child without ICPC approval creates legal problems which can potentially invalidate the adoption.

Cutting corners with ICPC can lead to nightmares. It's much more efficient financially and emotionally to have a professional process the ICPC work rather than to try and do it yourself or skip it altogether.

#30: ICPC Application Filed Upon Discharge from Hospital

An application for an interstate adoption may not be filed with the ICPC office until after the baby is discharged from the hospital and all pediatric medical reports, as well as numerous other legal documents, are included therein. This will enable the "receiving" state to understand any medical issues which accompany the baby from the "sending" state and also assures that the adoptive family is fully aware of any and all known medical issues.

#31: How ICPC Works, Basically

The ICPC examiners want to ensure that the baby is legally free to leave the state, and will therefore go over the package with a fine-toothed comb to confirm that consents were taken timely, the adoption professionals are properly licensed, the parental rights of any relevant parties are being correctly addressed, the adoptive family has proper clearances—criminal and other background checks—as well as a completed and acceptable home study.

ICPC will also check to confirm that a licensed social worker will supervise the proposed adoption after the family returns to their home until reports of post-placement activities are filed in court and the adoption is finalized.

#32: Finalization/Appearance at Hearing

Even if you do not live in the state where the baby was born, some states (i.e., Florida) permit the adoption to be finalized in the state of birth and the adoptive family may be permitted to appear at the final hearing on the adoption by telephone (as long as they are accompanied in their physical location by a Notary Public).

#33: ICWA

The Indian Child Welfare Act (ICWA) of 1978 contains important provisions to protect courts from inappropriately separating Native American children from their cultural roots.

The adoption of a child born to a mother with enough Native American heritage to qualify for tribal membership in the tribe by a non-tribe family is very risky as consent may be required from the tribe as well as the birth parents.

What constitutes "enough" Native American heritage to qualify for tribal membership varies widely from tribe to tribe. There is little if any uniformity in membership qualification, as each tribe makes its own qualification rules.

For example, to be considered for membership in the Seminole Tribe of Florida, one must have a minimum one-quarter Seminole blood; must prove in writing that he/she is directly related to a Florida Seminole who was on the 1957 Tribal

Roll; and must be sponsored for enrollment by a current member of the Tribe[3].

There are 562 federally-recognized tribes, and 562 different sets of criteria for membership. Does ICWA make you nervous? Good, it should, because it can apply <u>anytime</u>, even after the adoption is finalized, as you will see in item #34.

State courts do not have exclusive jurisdiction (authority) over the adoption of a child with Native American heritage—jurisdiction rests with the tribal court under ICWA.

Furthermore, the rules as to who qualifies for tribal membership vary widely from tribe to tribe, so it is oftentimes difficult to know whether tribal involvement is required at all.

> ***Case in Point:*** *A woman named Karen B. contacted us to help her place her unborn baby for adoption. She was only a couple of weeks away from delivery, so a variety of important legal wheels had to be set in motion in a fairly short period of time.*

---

[3] Seminole Tribe of Florida
http://www.SemTribe.com/FAQ/

In our interview with Karen, we became aware that although she was not a member of a Native American tribe, her mother had been a member of one of the local tribes and therefore she was fairly certain that she was at least eligible for membership. A review of the tribe's qualifications for membership quickly confirmed that Karen was, indeed, eligible, and 'contacting the tribe' was put on a list of things to do immediately.

Jeff Kasky called the tribe, which was and still is a large corporate entity, and navigated the maze of transfers until he was able to speak with the secretary for one of the tribe's attorneys. Jeff explained the situation, and advised the attorney that under ICWA he was required to seek the tribe's consent to the proposed adoption. Further, there was no time to waste, as Karen was due very soon. The lawyer advised that he would bring this up in his daily briefing with the tribe's chief and would get back to Jeff as soon as possible. Jeff faxed the proposed consent document to the lawyer for review, and awaited the tribe's response.

The next morning Jeff received a fax from the tribe's lawyer with the good news: The Chief, on behalf of the tribe, was happy to let the baby leave the tribe and be adopted by a couple who was unable to have children for themselves. However, there was a caveat: the Chief considered losing a potential tribe member to be a loss for his community, and wanted to receive TEN THOUSAND DOLLARS in exchange for his generous granting of consent to the adoption.

Jeff was then and still is unaware of how state criminal law juxtaposes with tribal sovereign immunity, but one thing was for sure—it looked an awful lot like an attempt to sell a baby. Fortunately, laws here in Florida are available in writing for anyone who wants to read them. Jeff made a copy of Fla. Stat. §63.212(1)(c), the statute that makes it illegal to exchange money or anything of value for the surrender of a minor child, and makes that act a FELONY, and faxed it immediately to the tribe's lawyer.

Within 45 minutes of the fax being sent, Jeff received by fax (and subsequently the original by Federal Express) a properly-executed consent by the Chief, releasing the child for adoption!

Would our local state attorney have prosecuted this case against the Chief or the tribe had they stuck to their guns? Who knows? We were very glad it didn't get there.

#34: ICWA Can Apply Anytime, Even After Finalization

An adoption which was processed and finalized in state court can be upset and reversed at seemingly any time in the event that the child is found to be the biological child of a member of a tribe and who is thus eligible him/herself for tribal membership or who is a person under age 18 who is a member of the tribe.

One hopes that as a child ages the court having jurisdiction over any case in which ICWA is being used to attempt to disrupt an adoptive placement will realize that the best interests of the child might not be served by removal from the adoptive home and replacement into the tribe.

#35: Tribal Criteria for Eligibility for Membership

These laws are oftentimes confusing and apply even if only one of the parents is eligible for membership in a federally-recognized tribe but isn't a member! Each tribe has its own criteria for membership eligibility, and oftentimes the biological parents do not themselves know which of his/her relatives are Native American, and whether their percentage of Native American blood makes them eligible for membership, and if so which tribe to which they are affiliated.

#36: ICWA Risk in Even Voluntary Placements

In most, if not all, non-ICWA adoptions, the consent of both parents (or a substitute for the unavailable father's consent) is necessary. As to children born out of wedlock, at least the birth mother's consent is required but not necessarily the birth father's consent. If the birth father's heritage falls under the scope of ICWA, his consent will be required if he has established or made an acknowledgment of his paternity under appropriate state law. Bottom line: even voluntary adoptive placements under ICWA have a high level of risk.

As a kind of safety backup in ICWA adoptions, there is a "good cause" exception in the law which provides that if the child's parents choose a non-Indian family to adopt the child, that preference can override the ICWA restrictive placement provisions even if suitable Indian parents are available. The "good cause" exception is handled on a case-by-case basis, but is uncertain at best.

CHAPTER 5

GENERAL COURT PROCEDURES AND STEP-PARENT ADOPTIONS

#37: After Consent is Signed, TPR

After a consent to adoption is signed, the birth parents' parental rights can only be terminated by a Judge in the jurisdiction where the adoption proceeding will take place.

The jurisdiction is usually the same as the location of the adoption entity's main office, but can also be the county in which the birth parents reside or the county in which the baby was born.

#38: Once Adoption Is Finalized

Once an adoption is complete, the adoptive family has the same rights, duties, and obligations to the child as they would have if they were the biological parents.

They can even place the baby for adoption with another family if they want to, as long as it's done through the proper legal channels. This happens more with international adoptions than with domestic adoptions in cases where the adoptive family finds itself unable and/or unwilling to deal with any social, emotional, and/or medical problems or issues which the child has.

#39: 90 days

In most cases, it takes 90 days or more from the birth of the child to the final hearing to complete an adoption. During the time between birth and finalization, a highly skilled and trained social service provider will report to the court and to the adoption agency or attorney as to how the family is adjusting to its new member, that the child has received appropriate paediatric care, and whether it is recommended that the adoption go forward as planned. If there is a problem, the child may be removed from the pre-adoptive home. This rarely happens if a favorable home study was issued prior to birth.

#40: The Best Interests of the Child

A Judge may render his/her decision in an adoption proceeding based on what is believed to be in the best interests of the child. The Judge will also rely on the adoption agency's consent, in its capacity as the child's legal guardian, to the adoption.

The best interests of the child is crucial but does not exist in a vacuum. There are decades of case law that direct a Judge as to how to deal with the concept of best interests.

#41: The Brightest Part of Most Judges' Day

In many jurisdictions, the Judges who hear adoption cases also hear family cases such as divorce, child custody, juvenile delinquency, and other unpleasant legal issues. To finalize an uncontested adoption and thus create a family for a child who may not have had one is the joy of their day!

If you are fortunate enough to adopt a child and you are able to be present in court for the hearing during which the Judge issues the Final Judgment of Adoption, be sure to bring a camera and ask the Judge to be part of a group picture. The Judges love it, and it's a great keepsake!

#42: Separation, Divorce and Death after Adoption

An adoption terminates the parent-child relationship between the child and the birth parents and creates a new relationship with the adoptive parents such that it gives rise to the obligation of the adoptive parents to support the child even if there is a subsequent dissolution or separation of the marriage of the adoptive parents. In other words, an adopted child is to be treated and provided with the same level of support, financial, educational and otherwise, as a biological child. Depending on matters of health, this support obligation can extend beyond the child's becoming an adult. This process also enables the child to have statutory rights to the estate of the parents on their death.

Further, for the purposes of inheritance, an adopted child has the very same legal rights to share in the parents' estate as does a biological child.

#43: Uncontested Step-Parent Adoption

An uncontested step-parent adoption is one of the easiest legal proceedings known to mankind, when the paperwork and procedures are created and completed correctly.

In that such an adoption results in the child becoming the legal child of the former step-parent (now the legal parent), step-parent adoption also vests the parents and the child with the rights, responsibilities and duties which would exist had the parent-child relationship been biological.

#44: Contested Step-Parent Adoption

The same cannot be said about a contested step-parent adoption where there may be issues of unpaid child support, custodial disagreements and, among others, visitation or time sharing rights. These can be contentious and unpre-dictable causing stress on all parties involved, regardless of who "wins" the case.

In a step-parent adoption, the rights of one parent are terminated when the spouse of the other parent adopts the child and becomes the child's legal parent. Whether the new spouse's adoption of the child is done with or without the consent of the other parent, the termination of parental rights and the establishment of legal parental rights in the adopting parent will not automatically extinguish the obligation of the other parent to pay back child-support (if there is a sum outstanding) and other agreed-upon or court-ordered expenses of the child through the date of the step-parent adoption.

The problems with step-parent adoptions arise when the birth father, who may or may not be paying child support, refuses to consent to the birth mother's husband adopting the child. Such refusal can impact the child's ability to get medical coverage and other benefits available to his/her step-father's children. These cases can easily get contentious and each one has its own idiosyncrasies.

Sometimes the birth father's refusal to cooperate is based on his honest desire to retain a legal relationship with his child, but oftentimes his refusal is based on a false sense of "machismo." Other times it's just to cause problems for the birth mother who just so happened to marry someone else.

__Case in point:__ Laura and her boyfriend Tom have a baby, Donna. Laura and Tom become yesterday's news a year later and Tom is court-ordered to pay for Donna's support. He fails to do so.

Several years later, Laura marries Bill. Bill does "the right thing" and starts step-parent adoption proceedings so he can become Donna's legal father and give her a sense of family security along with the love he has shown for her since day one. Tom refuses to consent to the step-parent adoption unless he gets a court order relieving him of his child support delinquencies, which Laura refuses to seek.

This case offers a Judge an excellent opportunity to blend legal concepts with common sense and to achieve a result which is both in the child's best interest and benefits society at large by providing a more secure and responsible home for a child.

In this case, the Judge considered whether Laura even had the ability to release Tom from his legal obligation to support Donna and likely concluded that she does not possess that right. If the story ended there, Bill would never be Donna's legal father and he would not be able to include her in, among other things, his health insurance plan and certain other employee benefits available to family members. Further, it was also deemed likely that Tom, the dead beat dad in this case, would likely not support Donna without considerable judicial intervention and even then he might not have had the resources or desire to do the right thing as ordered by the court.

The Judge exercised intellect and judicial discretion to achieve what was likely to be the best result for Donna and permitted Tom to be discharged from his child support obligation thus enabling Bill to adopt Donna and offer her the meaningful emotional, social, and financial stability that would have otherwise been unavailable to her.

#45: No Home Study in Step-Parent Adoption

No home study is required in most step-parent adoptions. The child may, depending on his/her age, be required to consent to the adoption. Since the petitioner in the adoption is the spouse of the child's parent, the parent must consent as well.

CHAPTER 6

AT THE HOSPITAL

#46: Most Anxious Time of the Whole Process

Without a doubt, the most anxious time for the prospective adoptive parents is the time when the birth mother is in the hospital, just about to or just having given birth to the baby.

Various state laws prohibit nurses and other healthcare providers and hospital staff-members from interfering with a birth mother's adoption plan. They cannot talk a woman into or out of making the placement. It is illegal in Florida for nurses, social workers and other healthcare employees to try to talk a woman into or out of placing her baby for adoption. Their dealings with the birth parents must be supportive and unbiased. They must simply support whatever decision their patient makes. Note: most nurses and hospitals are unfamiliar with these rules, and oftentimes violate them presumably with the intention of being supportive.

Case in point: Stephanie delivered on Monday at noon. She was in her hospital room awaiting Jeff's arrival, looking forward to executing the adoption consent and then going home. Jeff was approaching the hospital lobby when his phone rang. He could see from the caller ID that it was someone calling from within the hospital.

"Hi Stephanie!" exclaimed Jeff, shifting his briefcase from one hand to the other to avoid cell phone-related neck pain. "I'm coming up now!"

"Um, Mr. Cassidy, this is Betty Buzzkill, hospital social worker. I'm calling to advise you that Stephanie has changed her mind and is not placing her baby for adoption. She doesn't want you to come to the hospital to see her. She and her mother will be caring for her baby. Thank you, have a nice day."

"Wait, what?" said Jeff, "I just got off the phone with Stephanie less than 15 minutes ago! She was anxious to sign the paperwork

and leave the hospital. I'm here waiting for the court reporter now, and then we'll be on our way up. And by the way, not that it's a big deal, but it's Kasky, not Cassidy."

"Um, Mr. Cassidy, I request that you not attempt to come up to Stephanie's room. Hospital security will see you off the premises. Thank you, have a nice day."

"Wait! Don't hang . . . " Click. Betty Buzzkill had hung up the phone. Jeff was confused and on the verge of despondence. How could this have happened? He and the family had been there just last night, talking and laughing with Stephanie! This had to be a mistake.

Jeff dialed the direct number to Stephanie's hospital room. Busy. He called the hospital and asked the operator to put him through to the room. Still busy. He called the hospital again, and asked for the nurses' station closest to Stephanie's room.

"Nurses' station, this is Dawna."

"Hi Dawna, this is Jeff Kasky, I'm the lawyer handling the adoption for Stephanie, your patient in room . . . "

"I know who you are." said Dawna. *"I have been asked to tell you that that patient is not taking any calls."*

"I know," said Jeff. *"She had wanted her ex-boyfriend kept away from her while she was in the hospital, due to his history of violence towards her. But it's ok for you to put me through, I'm the lawyer working on her adop . . ."*

"Thank you, have a nice day." Click.

Jeff's cell phone rang almost immediately. It was Jillian, the prospective adoptive mom!

"Hi Jeff! We're so excited. Are you at the hospital yet? Has she signed the papers? Can we come and get our baby today? Our friends and family are so excited to meet him!"

Jeff's head was swimming. He couldn't believe this was happening . . . didn't know what to say.

"Jill, there is a problem over here and I'm trying to get to the bottom of it. I can't seem to get through to Stephanie, and the hospital social worker is telling me that there's not going to be an adoption. I don't know what's going on, but I'm working on it. Can I call you

back just as soon as I get to the bottom of this?"

"WHAT DID YOU SAY? NO ADOPTION? But, but, but . . . everything was fine last night! Oh no!" Jillian was bawling hysterically.

"Please just stand by and let me get to the bottom of this. There must be something else going on here, because the hospital staff is just plain shutting me out. I'll call you back."

Jeff tried Stephanie's room again but the line was still busy, so he texted to her cell phone.

"Hey! What's up up there? Hospital social worker won't let me come up. Phone's off hook or something. You ok?"

The reply came quickly. "I'm ok but I will kill this social worker! She tells me I'm gonna burn in hell if I give baby away. She took my phone off hook. Please come up!"

Oh sweet relief! Stephanie didn't change her mind after all, the problem was a hospital social worker with her own anti-adoption agenda! Although this is highly unusual as most social workers are a delight to work with, this was not the first nor would it be the last time that Jeff had to deal with obstructionist hospital employees who put *their own social/religious/moral agendas above the birth mother's adoption plan. But still he had to get upstairs.*

Jeff approached the security guard.

"ID please." Jeff presented his driver license. "You can't go upstairs."

"You don't understand, your patient in room . . . "

"I SAID YOU CAN'T GO UPSTAIRS!" interrupted the sweaty, badly-toupeed guard. "Step aside now."

Just then the elevator door opened. "Jeff, thank God you're here!" It was Stephanie! "I came down to meet you here in the lobby because the nurse told me she told me she wasn't letting you up. This place is a madhouse!"

"What happened?" Jeff asked.

Stephanie told the story: "Everything was fine until this morning. This nurse or social worker or whatever that I had never met before came into the room and said she had to 'counsel' me. I said no thank you but she sat down and told me that God wouldn't have given me a baby if he didn't want me to take care of it. I told her thank you, but I was taking care of him by giving him to someone who could give him the life I can't give him myself right now."

"Exactly!" said Jeff. "So what happened?"

"She wouldn't *%(@!^# leave me alone! She kept telling me that God would be mad if I gave my baby away, and that he would make me burn in hell for all eternity if I did this! Can you believe this wacko?!? Can we get the hell out of here?"

Just as Stephanie was catching her breath the court reporter Jeff had arranged showed up in the lobby. "I'll tell you what," said Jeff, "how bout we sit right here in the corner of the lobby and get this paperwork over with. Did you review it all last night after we left like I asked you to?"

"Yes," replied Stephanie. "Let's just get this done so I can get out of this crazy place."

Stephanie, Jeff, and the court reporter, along with two witnesses (as required by Florida law) from the hospital lobby, sat in a quiet corner and for the next twenty minutes reviewed, executed, and witnessed all of the post-delivery paperwork.

Afterwards, when the court reporter and the witnesses had been dismissed, and Stephanie's mother had picked her up and they were headed home, Jeff called the hospital administration office and spoke with the Director of Risk Management.

"Hi, this is Jeff Kasky. I'm a lawyer with a local adoption agency, and you're not going to believe what I'm about to tell you."

"Let me guess, does this have something to do with our social worker, Betty Buzzkill?" asked the voice on the other end of the phone.

"Well, obviously you already know the situation."

"No, not if it's a new one. Please come upstairs to my office and tell me what happened this time."

"Ok, I'll be there shortly," said Jeff, "but first there's one thing I have to do."

Jeff picked up the phone and called Jillian. "Are you sitting down?" He asked her.

"What's going on over there? We've been crying since the last time I spoke with you! Is

she keeping the baby?" Her voice was so thick you could cut it with a scalpel.

"All done!" said Jeff. "Papers are signed and Stephanie's on her way home! You can call her on her cell phone if you want. I don't know what time the baby will be discharged yet, but I'll let you know as soon as I know. This whole episode was caused by some nutcase social worker who was trying to prevent Stephanie from doing the adoption, for reasons that I'm trying to get to the bottom of."

"Oh my God! Is Stephanie ok?"

"She was a little shaken up by the whole thing but she seems fine now. I'm on my way upstairs to deal with this whole thing, drop the paperwork at the nurses' station so they know the baby is being placed for adoption, and to figure out the discharge time. I'll call you back."

Without interference at security, Jeff went through to the elevators, and upstairs to Risk Management.

As it turns out, the social worker and her husband, unable to conceive naturally or through IVF, had attempted unsuccessfully to adopt a child several times. She became bitter and angry, and decided to take it out on anyone she saw attempting to adopt or place a baby for adoption. This had been the third complaint that year against Betty Buzzkill, but it was also the last.

Based on numerous similar complaints, she was fired from the hospital.

#47: Birth Mother's Rights

Birth mothers have the same patient rights as any other person when seeking medical care in a hospital or doctor's office. This includes the right not to be belittled or to have their adoption decision questioned. If a nurse, medical assistant or office worker makes a woman feel uncomfortable, she has every right to ask that she not see that person again for care, or that she be referred to another healthcare provider.

#48: Access to Hospital Social Worker

Hospital protocol typically requires that a birth mother have access to the services of a social worker during her hospitalization. To the extent necessary, the social worker should only provide the birth mother with the information necessary to assist her in formulating a plan to either place the baby for adoption or take another course of action, and is precluded from offering personal opinions and feelings on what decision the birth mother should be making.

The birth mother's ultimate decision is generally based on a lifetime of events, good and bad, and it would be inappropriate and possibly illegal for a social worker to attempt to direct the birth mother in her decision-making process.

#49: Birth Mother's Choice

The birth mother can choose, subject to hospital protocol, whom she wants to be present with her in the delivery room and, of equal importance, whom she does not want to participate in the delivery or even visit her while she is hospitalized.

Subject to policies and procedures of the hospital, the birth mother can ask, for example, to include the prospective adoptive parent(s) to participate in the delivery if that is her and their desire. Typically, however, if either of the prospective adoptive parents is going to attend the delivery, it will be the adoptive mother while the adoptive father impatiently waits outside!

#50: Birth Mother's Rights

The birth mother has the right to privacy and confidentiality during her hospitalization. It is not unusual for the birth mother and the man in her life (if any) to have problems or to be in occasional disagreement regarding details of the adoption. If for that or any other reason, the birth mother does not want visits or phone calls from that man, she has every right to prevent him from calling or visiting, and can request that he be removed from the room should he be there creating any stress for her. Same goes for other family/friends.

#51: Epidurals

The term "epidural," when used in the context of pregnancy and delivery, refers to the administration of medicine via injection into the lower part of the spine of a woman for the purpose of mitigating the pain of childbirth. Epidurals are typically managed and administered by anesthesiologists in a hospital or medical center setting.

Epidurals are usually elective and not medically required. Therefore, they are not typically covered by medical insurance. Not everyone needs or benefits from having an epidural. However, if a pregnant woman requests or insists upon it, it's something that should be considered.

The procedure usually costs in the neighborhood of $1,000 - $1,500, and most of the medical practitioners who provide them require advance payment. Therefore, unless your adoption professional has an arrangement with the anesthesiologists practicing at the hospital where the birth is to take place, arrangements for an epidural should be made in advance.

Case in point: *My phone rang sometime around 4:00 am, as it so often does. I was living in Hollywood, Florida, and the call was from the nurses' station in the labor and delivery area of a hospital in Tampa, Florida, over 260 miles away.*

"Good morning, Mr. Kasky, this is Charge Nurse Carolyn at Tampa General."

Shaking off the cobwebs, "Good morning Carolyn. What's going on?"

"A woman is here in the hospital in labor, and everything is fine. She says she's a client of your agency. Her name is Kelly. She's here with her boyfriend Mark."

"Oh, ok, thanks for letting me know. Feel free to keep me posted, bye!" As much as I appreciate the hospital keeping me informed, I really love going back to sleep.

"Wait, don't hang up yet!" exclaimed Carolyn. "There is one issue which I need to discuss with you. Kelly is demanding an epidural. We have an anesthesiologist in the hospital this morning, but her practice requires payment in advance."

As a policy, One World Adoption Services will provide payment for a birth mother's epidural if she's requesting—or as in this case demanding—one.

"Can't they just bill us?" I asked. "We're a DCF-licensed agency. We pay our bills, and we're not going anywhere. I promise I'll send a check first thing tomorrow morning."

"No, I'm so sorry, but this doctor's practice requires payment in advance. They will take a check, though, but no credit cards. It doesn't have to be cash. The fee is $1,250."

It doesn't have to be cash! Wow, could you imagine if it DID have to be cash? There alongside all of the mysterious medical devices in the operating room would be an ATM, for your convenience!

I didn't say that, though. I replied, "I would love to be there in the next ten minutes to present you with a check, but it's 4:00 in the morning and I'm about 4 ½ hours away from you by car. Please either do the epidural and I will overnight a check to you tomorrow, or let me explain to the patient that no epidural will be done for her due to the doctor's practice's insistence that it be paid for in advance."

"Let me see if I can get the doctor to call you when she's in between patients. I'll call you back." Carolyn was gone, and I was wide-awake.

Two hours later, an hour after I had managed to fall back to sleep, the phone rang. It was Carolyn, calling to let me know that they got the needle in just in time, the epidural was administered, and the baby was born. Before her baby was one hour old the bill was already sitting in my fax machine, and we paid it the next day, as promised.

#52: Birth Certificate

At the time of birth, the birth mother may choose to name her baby and a birth certificate will be issued in the name chosen by the birth mother. The adoptive family will apply to change the child's name after the adoption is finalized in court and a new birth certificate will then be issued showing the adoptive family as the child's legal parents.

Many birth parents choose to use the first name chosen by the prospective adoptive parents and their own last name when the birth certificate representative comes to visit them in the hospital. If birth parents leave before filling out the birth certificate information or otherwise choose not to name the baby, the baby's legal name will be "Baby Boy/Girl [last name of birth mother]" until the adoption is finalized and the baby is given the name chosen by the adoptive family.

#53: Early Bonding

After consent papers are signed, it is common for the prospective adoptive family to spend time with the baby in the nursery. This is a time when bonding takes place notwithstanding the un-certainty as to the overall outcome of the adoption (i.e., will the birth mother revoke her consent if state law allows). This is, of course, an emotionally charged time because of the un-certainty and it is critical for the prospective adoptive family to listen closely and attentively to the advice and counsel given by their adoption professionals. If a parent is permitted to revoke the consent, hearts will be broken.

#54: Adoption Status

In the garden-variety adoption, the baby is discharged to the agency or lawyer who may serve as the baby's legal guardian until the adoption is concluded. At the time of discharge, it is common for the adoptive family to be present in the nursery to receive the newborn instructions typically delivered by the highly skilled nurses in the newborn or other nursery from which the baby will be discharged. This, too, is an exciting and emotional event but it must be kept in perspective should the state in which the adoption is taking place permit revocation of the consent at a later date. Soon after discharge (frequently 48 hours after birth), the baby should have a first visit with a private paediatrician and the family will have all discharge medicals with them to start the baby's new medical history chart.

CHAPTER 7

CONSENT PROCEDURE

#55: Birth Mother Consent

A Birth Mother may not sign a valid consent to place her child for adoption until after the child's birth. In Florida a birth father may, however, relinquish his parental rights prior to the birth of the child.

Each state has its own rules as to the waiting period after birth before a woman can sign papers placing the baby for adoption, but only in the rarest cases that are very few and very far between can a woman sign a valid consent for adoption prior to the birth of the child.

In Florida, a birth mother may sign a consent to adoption on the earlier of the day she is notified of her discharge from the hospital or 48 hours after the birth of the child. Each state designates the time-frame for when consents may be executed, but situational flexibility is often allowed based on the possibility of the birth mother leaving the hospital prior to signing consents and potential subsequent inability to locate her.

#56: Judge or Court Reporter Not Necessary

A consent to adoption need not be signed in the presence of either a Judge or a court reporter although the latter is a preferred method of documenting the execution of the consent. It is a way to directly inquire of the birth mother whether she is signing the documents knowingly and voluntarily and, in Florida, to confirm that she understands that the consent is irrevocable (unless secured by fraud or duress).

Most states do not require that the consent be signed in the presence of a court reporter. However, best practice would be the use of a court reporter for the Consent signing whenever possible to avoid a subsequent "he-said, she-said" if a claim is made that the consent was obtained under duress or was based on mis-representations. The extra couple of hundred bucks for a court reporter can make all the difference in the world if any party subsequently contests the validity of the consents.

#57: Birth Mother Need Not Relinquish in Her State

A birth mother is allowed to deliver and sur-render the baby in a state other than her state of residence, as long as she's not traveling to avoid certain laws in her jurisdiction.

If the birth mother wishes to travel to and place the baby for adoption in Florida, just to avoid the laws of her state regarding either parental rights or financial support (for example), the adoption, if challenged, may be subject to the laws of the state of the birth mother's residence. On the other hand, if the birth mother is from outside of Florida and travels to Florida to deliver for reasons unrelated to her state's adoption laws, Florida law can be applied.

#58: Entity = Legal Guardian

In some states, a licensed adoption agency or child placing agency will become, for all practical purposes, the Legal Guardian of the child once the birth mother's consent to place the child for adoption is signed.

The baby will have a legal guardian at all times during the various stages of the adoption process. Rights and responsibilities for a child are transferred from one party to another without interruption.

At the time of birth, the birth mother has parental rights to the baby. Upon signing consents, the rights transfer immediately to the adoption entity or to the adoptive family, depending on the type of adoption and the laws and procedures of the state in which the adoption is taking place. Sometimes there will be a hearing several weeks later in which a judge "orders" the termination of parental rights of the birth parents, but this "order" is more like an official acknowledgement of what has already occurred. Lastly, the adoption entity will transfer its rights to the adoptive family when the adoption is finalized.

Each of these transfers is subject to legal challenge, primarily based on whether the party consenting to have his/her/its rights terminated and transferred to another party had those rights to transfer in the first place.

#59: Baby Goes Home

Although the baby typically goes home from the hospital with the adoptive family, there is a legal process that remains to be completed to make the adoptive family the legal parents of the child. After parental rights are terminated, there must be a final hearing to conclude the adoption.

Many adoption professionals will have the prospective adoptive family sign some type of "At-Risk" and/or "Guardianship" letter acknowledging that they're taking the baby as sort of glorified baby-sitters, and that there's work to do and time must pass before they become the legal parents of the child. Again, each state has a law stating when an adoption can be finalized.

#60: Adoption-Related Emancipation

In Florida, a birth mother over the age of 14 may sign a consent to adoption without parental consent or a legal guardian's consent.

A birth mother 14 years old or younger may not sign a consent to adoption without the consent of a parent, legal guardian, or court-appointed guardian.

It happens too often that a birth mother, birth father, or both are under 14 years old or younger. In those cases they cannot give their consent for adoption in many jurisdictions without parental consent, a legal guardian's consent, or court approval.

Even though they are not legally adults, some jurisdictions consider birth parents who are 14 years old or older emancipated for the purpose of adoption consents. Their parents need not be notified and have no rights to the child being placed for adoption or for information of any kind about the adoption.

#61: Birth Father's Consent

A birth father's consent to adoption may be executed at any time after the birth of the child to be placed for adoption. There is no statutory waiting period for birth father consent in Florida.

Some states allow the birth father to sign a document prior to the child's birth in which he essentially consents to the adoption of the as-yet unborn child. In Florida the document is called Affidavit of Non-Paternity. Even a legal father (i.e., married to the mother) can sign this document. It essentially waives the need for the birth father or legal father to consent to the adoption after the birth of the child.

However, if the birth father wishes to sign a consent to adoption as opposed to the Affidavit of Non-Paternity, he can do so any time after the birth of the child, and it becomes immediately irrevocable (absent fraud or duress).

#62: Influence of Meds or Alcohol

It is important to ascertain that the birth parents are not under the influence of medications, drugs, or alcohol at the time the consent is signed. If they are, the validity of the consent can be brought into question and it may be invalidated.

Good practice for an adoption professional would be to advise the birth mother and the medical care givers that the birth mother should be off of narcotics for at least four hours prior to signing the Consent. If it would be medically inadvisable to withhold those meds, or if the birth mother has any objection to being off the medications, the prudent thing to do is to wait until all parties agree that it's appropriate before presenting the Consent to the birth mother for signature.

#63: Two Witnesses and a Notary

A consent to adoption must generally be signed by the birth mother in the presence of two witnesses and a Notary Public (who cannot be a witness).

The birth mother has the right to choose at least one of the witnesses to the Consent. If she chooses in advance and that witness is not present for the execution of the Consent, it is permissible to substitute another witness, as long as the birth mother had the opportunity to pick at least one of the two. She may also waive this right.

CHAPTER 8

SPECIAL NEEDS ADOPTIONS AND SUBSIDIES

#64: Special Needs Includes Siblings

"Special needs" adoptions include sibling groups (even if the kids are healthy), children with special medical needs, children with special emotional needs, children with learning challenges, and children with a diagnosis of physical and/or emotional disabilities. There is almost always some kind of assistance, sometimes including a guarantee of college tuition, available from state, local and federal governmental sources for the adoption of special needs children. Accessing such resources is an area requiring highly-trained professionals but if a child qualifies for such benefits, it's well worth the effort.

Do you want to make a crucial difference in the life of a child? Adopt a child who might not be what many would view as the "ideal" adoption situation. Consider adopting a sibling group or a child with special needs. Extra training is often-times required, and there's nothing easy about the entire process, but if you want to change the world one person at a time, this is a great way to start!

> ***Case in point:*** *In the late '90s we had the pleasure of helping a couple named Becky and Jim. Becky was approximately five months pregnant with twin girls, and had delivered a set of twin girls just ten months prior to her involvement with us. Those girls were taken into protective custody by the Department of Children and Families im-mediately after birth due to Becky's lifestyle and substance abuse issues. Jim was said to be the father of both pregnancies.*
>
> *During the course of the second pregnancy, Becky and Jim decided that they wanted to meet the parents who were expecting to adopt the new set of twins. The parents, Nigel and Amy, flew to Tampa from their home in*

Southern California, very nervous to meet this couple about whom they had been hearing so much. Becky, for her part, seemed a little too relaxed and confident. It seemed to me that she had something up her sleeve. We met at a diner in Plant City, Florida, the city of Becky's and Jim's residence.

During the meeting Becky dropped a bomb. She told Nigel and Amy that she was sick of fighting what she perceived was going to be a losing battle against the Department, and wanted to relinquish custody of the first set of twins to them, so that both sets of twin girls could be legal as well as biological siblings, and would grow up knowing each other.

Nigel and Amy knew of the situation with the twins in DCF care, but they were not expecting this huge bombshell. Their jaws simultaneously dropped and they were very literally speechless! After what seemed like an eternity of shocked silence, Nigel spoke first.

"Wow!" was all he could manage to croak out of his dry mouth.

Amy burst into tears and managed to choke out that yes, they would absolutely love and would be honored to be the parents of all four girls!

All eyes turned to me. Was it possible to do this? What about the foster family in which the twins had been living for the past ten months? Would they have some kind of say in the decision? Did Becky have the legal right to choose the parents of the twins if they had been in the Department's care for all this time?

Current Florida law specifically allows us to "intervene" in the Department's case when the birth parent(s) consent and their parental rights haven't yet been terminated. The theory behind this is that until and unless the Court terminates a parent's rights, that parent still holds those rights and can therefore transfer them pursuant to the rules of adoption law. However, this concept had not been codified—or written into the law—back in the '90s. I knew that this sort of placement had been done before, but I also knew that it would require the cooperation of multiple entities and parties, including DCF, the Guardian ad Litem assigned to the twins, the dependency lawyers assigned to Becky and Jim individually, and, of course, the Court itself.

The next day I started making calls. I was shocked and delighted to find that the DCF caseworker assigned to the twins was accessible and cooperative, which is not necessarily a "given." With Becky and Jim's permission, she filled me in on the status of the case. The best news of all was that the family who had been providing foster care to the twins since the day of their discharge from the hospital was not interested in adopting them! They would not likely have had legal rights superior to those of the birth couple, but the fewer people you have to disappoint in a case like this the better.

Shortly thereafter, after all parties had had the opportunity to absorb the magnitude of what they were trying to accomplish and were still interested in moving forward, I took the consents of Becky and Jim as to the twins, and began taking action to advise the Court and all relevant parties that the birth parents were transferring their parental rights to this home study-ready, agency-approved adoptive family.

This was one of those rare cases where the stars aligned and everyone seemed to want to cooperate. It was not long before DCF, the twins' guardian, the birth parents' lawyers, the foster parents, and the Court were all in agreement that the best interest of the twins would be served by allowing them to be placed for permanent adoption with Nigel & Amy, and that's exactly what happened.

Three months later, Becky delivered her second set of twins, and she and Jim signed adoption consents in favor of Nigel & Amy. After an extended stay in the neonatal intensive care unit due to prematurity and withdrawal from Becky's opiate habit, the new twins went home to be with their biological sisters and their new parents!

Post-script: We keep in touch with Nigel and Amy, who have been providing Becky & Jim with pictures of both sets of twins since the beginning.

The oldest of the girls has been arrested three times, and is a habitual runaway. Her twin has almost uncontrollable anger issues and has been kicked out of several private schools for fighting.

Neither of the younger set of twins is having any noticeable difficulty, aside from the familial turmoil of living with the other two.

Post-post script: Two years after the events described above, Becky's sister Robin contacted us to place her two young sons, ages 6 and 7, whom she was unable and/or unwilling to continue to parent. They were adopted by Nigel's sister and her husband, who live in close proximity to Nigel and Amy. The adoption of those two boys was uneventful, although one of them has since died in a car chase with police. Seriously.

#65: 100,000+ Special Needs Children Await Placement

At any given time there are over 100,000 children with varying degrees and types of "special needs" sitting in foster care awaiting placement right here in the United States of America. Consider this before undertaking an effort to adopt from overseas.

Also consider the fact that children who are available for adoption from outside of the U.S. do not necessarily and automatically come without their own issues and special needs! Why is a 3-year-old in an orphanage in Russia? Is it because that child comes from a loving home and his mother made healthy choices during her pregnancy? I'm going to put my money on "NO," especially since I've been there and seen it.

#66: Federal Law Gives Much Subsidy Control to the State

Federal laws governing programs which provide assistance to special needs children vest in the states much of the discretion as to who qualifies for such assistance and to what extent. There are many laws, rules, regulations, and procedures which come into play and it is best left to either a highly qualified social worker, attorney or other professional to help decipher what programs correspond to the needs of the child for whom the application is made. It can be a dizzying experience to navigate these waters and coordinate the benefits without the help of a seasoned professional.

#67: Which Kids Qualify for Subsidies?

Typically, to qualify for a federal, state and/or local subsidy, a child must have one or more factors which would make it reasonable to conclude that a conventional adoption without financial assistance is unlikely and basically unavailable due to the relatively small number of prospective adoptive parents who are interested in adopting a child with that given child's affliction, whatever it may be. Further, it must also be concluded that the state tried, unsuccessfully, to place the child for adoption without financial assistance. Lastly, it must be concluded that it would be in the best interest of the child to not be returned to the biological parents of the child.

#68: Benefits Can Continue Indefinitely

If a special needs child who is receiving an adoption subsidy turns 18 and is eligible for SSI (Supplemental Security Income), Medicaid and other financial benefits can continue indefinitely, even if the adoptee is still living in the adoptive parents' home, as follows:

Sec. 307. Continuation of Eligibility for Adoption Assistance Payments on Behalf of Children with Special Needs Whose Initial Adoption Has Been Dissolved.

(a) Continuation of Eligibility—Section 473(a)(2) of the Social Security Act (42 U.S.C. 673 (a)(2)) is amended by adding at the end the following: "Any child who meets the requirements of subparagraph (C), who was determined eligible for adoption assistance payments under this part with respect to a prior adoption, who is available for adoption because the prior adoption has been dissolved and the parental rights of the adoptive parents have been terminated or because the child's adoptive parents have died, and who fails to meet the requirements of subparagraphs (A) and (B) but would meet such requirements if the child were treated as if the child were in the same financial and other circumstances the child was in the last time the child was determined eligible for adoption assistance payments under this part and the prior adoption were treated as never having occurred, shall be treated as meeting the requirements of this paragraph for purposes of paragraph (1)(B)(ii)."

(b) Applicability—The amendment made by subsection (a) shall only apply to children who are adopted on or after October 1, 1997.

#69: Denials of Benefits Can Be Appealed

Adoption subsidies are available for families that adopt newborn infants as well as those that adopt children from a state foster care program. When applying for any such subsidy, be aware that a denial does not always mean that benefits will not be forthcoming; rather, it means that the applicant will have to demand a "fair hearing" on the matter and will thus be given the opportunity to make a personal appearance before a committee whose responsibilities include making subsidy determinations including the availability of funding for the specific situation.

Some allegations that constitute grounds for a fair hearing include:

- relevant facts regarding the child were known by the State agency or child-placing agency and not presented to the adoptive parents prior to the finalization of the adoption
- denial of assistance based upon a means test of the adoptive family
- adoptive family disagrees with the determination by the State that a child is ineligible for adoption assistance
- failure by the State agency to advise potential adoptive parents about the availability of adoption assistance for children in the State foster care system
- decrease in the amount of adoption assistance without the concurrence of the adoptive parents
- denial of a request for a change in payment level due to a change in the adoptive parents circumstances

Case in point (contributed by Margaret T. Snider, MSW) The Story of Jessamyn: On February 8, 2010, an application for supplemental security income was filed on behalf of Jessamyn, an infant born on December 27, 2009, with congenital scoliosis, T8 abnormality and severe hip dysplasia. She was also diagnosed with Klippel-Feil Syndrome (KFS), which consisted of congenital fusions of the cervical vertebrae. Furthermore, the child underwent therapy for torticollis and thumb in hand deformity requiring the use of a neoprene brace. Therefore, her first year of life required regular orthopedic care, therapy, and assistive devices to improve her physical functioning. In spite of these therapeutic interventions, Jessamyn continued to have a significant spinal deformity, and at 17 months of age, her spine curved completely. She could not walk or run due to dislocated hips and the use of a brace.

At the time of initial application for disability in February, 2010, Jessamyn was 6 weeks old, and there was insufficient medical documentation of her physical and congenital impairments. As she became older, medical documentation was submitted to the Social Security office.

An initial denial of Jessamyn's claim occurred on March 1, 2010, stating that because she was not disabled or blind under Social Security rules, she did not qualify for payments on the claim.

Individuals at the Social Security office where the claim was filed urged that steps be taken to appeal the decision. At our request, the Social Security office filed the appeal within 14 days of the initial denial of benefits. As the months went by, they continued to assist and hasten the appeals process. A second denial of benefits occurred in October, 2010, with a statement by the State agency's medical consultants that additional medical verifications provided by specialists involved in Jessamyn's care did not conclusively rule out that Jessamyn might someday grow into being a physically well-functioning person.

An appellate hearing was finally arranged for June 2, 2011, 16 months after the initial request for benefits was filed. At that hearing, the presiding Judge, after considering the evidence of record, determined that the State agency's medical consultants' assessments did not adequately consider the combined effect of Jessamyn's impairments. Further, he found Jessamyn's medically determinable impairments could reasonably be expected to produce the alleged symptoms, and the intensity, persistence and limiting effects of these symptoms were generally credible.

The Judge made a fully favorable decision and granted Social Security Disability benefits for Jessamyn, effective the date of initial application, February 8, 2010.

Jessamyn was born with several severe and serious congenital problems. Also, her birth mother, who was homeless, did not want her and relinquished her for adoption the day after she was born. During Jessamyn's stay in the neonatal intensive care unit after birth, a crucial and important coincidence occurred. The NICU nurse assigned to care for Jessamyn fell in love with her, contacted the adoption agency and inquired about the possibility of adopting her.

This woman was a 20 year pediatric R.N., married with four teenage children. Prior to meeting Jessamyn, she had no plans for any more children. She was also an assertive advocate for Jessamyn's needs. When Jessamyn was discharged from the hospital, she was placed for adoption with this nurse, her husband and four children. The husband

and children were thrilled and happy to have Jessamyn in their home, fell in love with her, and eleven months later, completed their adoption. In spite of her physical disabilities, Jessamyn is smart, quick to learn, and has an effervescent, gregarious personality. She engages everyone she comes into contact with in a most positive manner.

Good fortune was also on Jessamyn's side during the application and resolution phase regarding her Social Security Disability benefits. The two government employees processing her application were caring, professional persons who took a keen interest in Jessamyn's situation, encouraged and assisted in advocating for an appeals hearing after two denials by the State medical team. Last, but not least important, the Judge assigned to Jessamyn's case had a granddaughter with a very similar diagnosis, making him unusually sensitive to her case.

As a footnote, in March of 2012, Jessamyn underwent a successful 16 hour surgical intervention to straighten her back and give support through expanding rods to several of her cervical vertebrae. Physicians and specialists involved in this operation told the adoptive parents her scoliosis was the worst and most severe they had ever seen, and without surgical intervention, she would probably have died before she was three years old.

#70: Not Just Anyone Can Adopt Special Needs Children

Not just any family will qualify to adopt a child or sibling group with special needs.

Every time it looks like the world is going down the tubes and people don't seem to care about anything but themselves, we are reminded of the various couples and singles who contact our Agency only wanting to adopt a child with special needs. Typically, they're professionals—sometimes with a medical background—who are also empty-nesters with the financial and emotional ability to take care of a child who wouldn't be considered most families' first choice as an adoptive child.

However, as big as one's heart and as genuine as one's mission to help might be, the varying degrees of "special needs" have correlating varying degrees of skills and training that must be taught, learned and demonstrated to get to the point of approval for these adoptions.

The most severe special needs people are a full-time, lifetime project. If you believe in heaven, this is your sure-fire way to get there. Just please-oh-please be sure you know what you're getting into, because to have to disrupt one of these adoptions due to a family's unpreparedness would be a tragedy, despite the genuineness of their original intentions.

#71: Assistance Must Remain in Place State-to-State

When a Special Needs child is being adopted by a family which resides in a state other than the state in which the child resides, there are federal and state laws which provide that adoption assistance programs will remain in place for the child regardless of the state of residency of the adoptive family. Further, all levels of services available to the child in his/her state of residency will be available should the adoptive family relocate. This is an area where it is best to have documentation of all state programs which the child qualifies for along with a stipulation that if the new state of residence does not offer certain of those services available in the state from which the child moves, the state from which the child moves will help the family identify the sources of such services and will enable them to progress towards having such services paid for in the new state of residency.

#72: Family Considerations

Finally, under this Special Needs category, I am reminded of the sermon given at every final hearing by one of Broward County, Florida's most highly respected Judges, Judge John A. Fruschiante, Ret., who reminds each family that while they certainly need to allocate much of their time, attention, energy, and love to the adopted child (special needs or not), they must also focus on maintaining intact the structural foundation of their marriage and their inter-personal relationship.

It is not a sign of weakness to seek outside help to achieve goals such as: dealing with the inevitable marital tensions which can be created by having a special needs child; the stress caused by coping with the challenges, joys, and disap-pointments which may become daily events and not letting such stresses cause problems with the rest of the family; the ability to continue to nurture any other children in your home with your attention, love, and guidance; and many other events which challenge your desire to have as functional and normal a family life as is possible. Outside help can assist you in keeping everything in proper perspective and should be used when needed.

Your community resources may direct you to services which can provide the kind of information you may find helpful in raising a special needs child. If not, the internet will expose you to videos, web sites, books, social workers experienced in special needs adoptions, support groups and many other resources for obtaining some outside assistance to help you successfully maintain your family structure while providing the special needs child with that something extra that he/she needs.

The need for experienced and sensitive counseling is profound when a family adopts a special needs child who will most definitely require substantially more of a family's time, attention, and energy than would a child without special needs. In a recent case, a family devoted virtually every waking hour to the child's special needs and it was apparent to our social worker that they were approaching burn-out. That being the assessment, the social worker mandated that the family not only make every effort to resume their normal routine but also required that the family identify a responsible guardian to relieve the family for a few hours at least twice weekly so they could have some time together to go to dinner and a movie or some such activity all the while knowing that the child was in good hands. This demand by our social worker was coupled with a strong recommendation that the family have a local family therapist as a back-up to the social worker who does not live in the family's community. The recent reports suggest that trying to be as normal a family as they can be has greatly reduced the family's stress and enabled them to be more relaxed yet responsible parents.

CHAPTER 9

OPENNESS DURING AND FUTURE CONTACT AFTER ADOPTION

#73: Adopted Child is Child of New Parents

Once an adoption is completed, the child becomes the child of the adoptive parents in all respects. Adoption files are confidential and are sealed by the court. Therefore, an adopted child's access to information about the birth parents is typically limited to the information which the adoptive parents received from the adoption professional during the adoption process.

With social media what it is today, and with internet access so easily available, the opportunities available to an adopted child to gain information about the birth parents has increased significantly. Only time will tell whether this is beneficial or detrimental to adopted children in general. There will be horror stories and there will be heartwarming tales of beautiful reunions.

We have found that some adoptive families who come to us not intending to have any degree of openness in their adoption but who then choose to be more flexible have positive adoption experiences and thus are glad they agreed to some degree of openness. Don't draw any bottom lines until you've considered the value of some degree of openness. Remain flexible.

#74: Sealed File Means Court Order or 'Good Cause'

Once the court file is sealed, the contents are unavailable to anyone except by court order based on a demonstration of "good cause." This is to protect both the adoptive family and the birth parents from unwanted intrusion by the other and is a recognition of the rights to privacy of all parties involved in the adoption.

Depending on the jurisdiction, the courts have the ability in some situations to open these files, usually for "good cause," such as the urgent need for medical information.

"Good cause" usually relates to obtaining necessary information to address the medical or psychiatric needs of the child under circumstances where such information is not otherwise available and may only appear in the original adoption records. "Good cause" is not interpreted to mean because a child wants to find and reunite with his/her biological parents.

#75: Exposure During "Open" Adoption Scenarios

How much exposure is the right amount of exposure when you're undertaking an "open" adoption, or an adoption plan in which there is personal contact between the birth and adoptive parent(s)?

The answer to this question will be different for every case, based on the personalities of the various parties. People who are willing to enter into an "open" adoption-type arrangement should, by nature, be reasonably social just by virtue of the fact that they want a degree of openness. With this in mind, how do you remain neutral enough to prevent your exposure with the "other side" from torpedoing your adoption plan? Start by making every effort to NOT over-expose yourself. The more comfortable you get with the other side the more likely you are to let your guard down and do or say something that might be offensive or contrary to the beliefs of the person to whom you're speaking.

> *Case in point: At their respective requests, we introduced a set of birth parents to a set of adoptive parents. Subsequent to enjoying a meal together with Robert facilitating the conversation, the two sets of parents wanted to take a walk in the mall together, so they could bond between the four of them.*
>
> *That afternoon the birth mother called Robert and he could tell she'd been crying. He asked her what was wrong, and she replied that while walking past the pet store in the mall, the adoptive father mentioned that he wasn't a pet person, and that he had had allergies to animals as a child. The birth mother, who was a dog lover, was devastated at the prospect of her child being raised without a family dog.*

Is that a big deal? It was to her! Eventually it was smoothed over by the adoptive father re-examining his priorities and agreeing to purchase a small dog. Everyone lived happily ever after.

#76: No Right or Wrong with Post-Adoption Contact

Times are changing. Professionals differ as to whether it is wise for the birth parents to have access to information about the child after the adoption. There is no right or wrong when it comes to the issue of post-adoption contact. Even if the birth parents and the adoptive family agree to share information in the future, there is no guarantee that such an agreement is enforceable or in the child's best interests.

> *Case in point: We were contacted by a woman in Orlando who was pregnant and requesting help to place her baby for adoption. Her story was amazing, sad and inspirational.*
>
> *Alaine is from The Congo on the continent of Africa, and at the time of our work with her was living in Orlando and working at an African restaurant in the EPCOT Center. She was a little over 6 feet tall, slim and athletic, and would be the first thing you'd think of if*

someone asked you to imagine an African Princess.

Alaine was present in her home when it was stormed by a rebel army. She managed to hide in the fireplace and she watched as the invaders slaughtered her parents, brothers and sisters with machetes. She remained hidden for hours until she was sure that the murderers had left her village, and then emerged as one of only a small handful of survivors of the massacre.

Eventually the UN sent trucks to the area to look for survivors, and she and the others were driven hours across roadless lands to a refugee camp with many thousands of other survivors from across the region. The conditions were deplorable, with thousands sleeping on the bare ground under and around tents. Food was scarce, as much of it was being stolen by UN personnel and sold to regional warlords. The camp had no plumbing or bathroom facilities. Besides all that, Alaine was having to fight men off, and was assaulted and nearly raped almost every day she was there, for three full months.

Word of a pending raid on the refugee camp by the rebels began to spread. Alaine knew she had to get out of there, so she and her best friend snuck away one night and decided to just take their chances in the open. They walked for weeks, eating anything they could find, sleeping where and when they could, and hiding from the rare passing motorist. Eventually they were able to get to a fairly-organized city, where they were taken in by American charity workers and nourished back to health.

The Americans helped Alaine and her friend apply successfully for humanitarian visas, and the girls both traveled to Orlando, Florida to attend college and work at Walt Disney World under a Disney scholarship/work program. They found a vibrant Congolese community in central Florida and socialized when they weren't working or studying. Alaine even found a long-lost uncle whom she thought had been killed in the war.

Shortly thereafter Alaine was raped by that uncle and became pregnant with the baby she was placing for adoption. Unaware of how law enforcement worked in the US, Alaine was afraid to call the police lest they come and abuse her further, which is what she could reasonably have expected in Africa. As soon as she found out she was pregnant, she realized that she didn't want to keep the baby and would rather have it raised by a loving family who was unable to have children for themselves.

We matched Alaine with Asher and Camryn, a married couple from New Mexico. At Alaine's request, Asher and Camryn traveled to Orlando, anxious to meet this African Princess.

The three of them got along like they had been best friends for years! Lunch lasted through dinner, and nobody wanted to leave. They kept in touch by phone until they returned for the birth of the baby which was like a family reunion.

Asher and Camryn are now the parents of an unusually tall and athletic, beautiful and smart young girl who is fully aware of her heritage, but the story doesn't end there. Asher & Camryn and their daughter visit Orlando at least twice each year, where they spend the weekend with Alaine and her husband! Alaine is a 2nd year law student in Orlando, and is presently interning at a nearby county's courthouse in the domestic violence unit. She still works part-time at Disney World, where she met her husband, who works in Disney's accounting office.

They are not yet expecting, but are planning their first child for the Fall of 2013.

#77: Adoption Reunion Registry

To circumvent some of these post-adoption access to information issues, many states, including Florida, have what is referred to as an adoption reunion registry which is essentially a data bank into which the birth parents may enter their names and addresses in the hopes that the child, at age 18, will seek them out. If the child seeks out the birth parents and there is current information in the registry about their where-abouts, problem solved. The registry is optional and the birth parents who register may, based on changes in their circumstances, change their minds and withdraw from the registry and thus remain anonymous.

Case in point: Gregg, a lawyer we knew, was adopted as a newborn. When he was in his mid-30s Gregg decided to try to track down his birth parents for a reunion. Through a private investigator who we know, Gregg was able to track down a name and telephone number for his birth mother. He asked us whether we thought he should make the call, and we discussed the pros and cons.

The pros were that she could possibly fill in some of the pieces of his life's puzzle and give him some insight as to his roots and heritage. He had no known medical problems or health or emotional issues, and was adopted by a family filled with love, support and happiness. The cons were mainly that he might learn something unfortunate or unsettling that he would rather not have known. It was also possible that his birth mother had closed that chapter of her life and was not interested in reliving that part of her past. It was of course possible that his birth mother had started a new family altogether, and perhaps had not shared her adoption experience with them.

Gregg chose to go forward with calling, assuming that his birth mother, Marci, would be delighted to hear from him and would welcome a reunion after 30+ years. Boy, was he wrong.

Gregg reached Marci on the phone and with trembling voice introduced himself as the baby she placed for adoption 30-something years ago. By the look on his face (we were both there for this) he clearly expected her to go off the charts with joy and excitement. However, Gregg's face melted when his introduction was countered with a cool "Ok."

Now 50 years old, Marci was not in the least bit interested in rehashing that time in her life. She told Gregg that she had a family of her own now, along with a successful career, and was not up for the meeting/reunion which he proposed. However, Gregg pushed. He pushed and pushed and pushed until finally Marci said, "Fine, we'll get together one time if it'll make you happy."

As the big day approached, Gregg was positively aflutter with excitement. He just knew deep down inside that he'd be able to win her over, and have some type of as-yet undefined friendship or relationship with his new friend Marci.

Gregg met Marci at a chain restaurant for lunch. Marci was cold, but answered Gregg's questions. There was nothing helpful or important she had to add. Gregg was dying for some connection, but Marci was giving him nothing.

Finally, Gregg advised Marci that he had become a fairly successful lawyer, and that if there's anything she needed he would welcome the opportunity to repay her for the gift she gave him. Marci's eyes lit up.

Although Marci had told him otherwise, she admitted that she had done nothing to obtain an education, and was presently out of work, without a vehicle, without a husband or even a significant relationship, and facing eviction. She had been living boyfriend-to-boyfriend, and had been selling pain pills to make ends meet. This offer of help was the break she had been looking for!

For the next three months Marci called Gregg 3-5 times each week for everything from help with groceries and rent to bills for a broken tooth and more. Gregg became Marci's personal bottomless ATM. Finally enough was enough. He drew the line and stuck to it, and discontinued all contact with Marci. She presumably moved on to suck the life out of someone else.

When this episode ended, Gregg had extremely negative feelings about what had happened between him and Marci. In retrospect, he readily admitted that his being a successful lawyer made him an easy target for financial exploitation by a desperate person, biological relationship aside.

The advantages versus disadvantages of finding a birth parent are unpredictable until it actually happens.

We recommend that parties wishing to seek a reunion first contact a social worker or therapist with experience in adoption and reunion. It is crucial that you flesh out not only the issues that can come up as a result of a reunion, but those that are creating the need to seek a reunion in the first place. Further, it will be important to explore strategies as to how to deal with reunions that fail, either because the other party cannot be located, or the other party refuses to engage in a reunion.

#78: Grandparental Rights

What about grandparents? Do they have any visitation or other rights to the adopted child? In the case of newborns, the answer is generally "no" because the courts and the statutes typically protect the privacy of the adoptive family. So, generally, the grandparents have no visitation rights and when the adoption is finalized by the new family it effectively marks the termination of all rights of all members of the family which placed the baby for adoption, including grandparents, aunts, etc. While this may seem difficult for the grandparents to deal with, it is based on the need for the new family to have privacy and the unfettered status as legal parents of the child adopted.

#79: Grandparent Rights—Older Child

There may be some state exceptions to the complete elimination of the rights of grand-parents (check your state laws) when a child is adopted by non-relatives. For example, in Florida, if a child has lived with a grandparent for at least 6 months within the 24 month period preceding the filing of a petition to terminate parental rights pending the adoption, the grand-parents will at least be given notice that the grandchild is to be adopted and presumably the opportunity to contest the adoption. Whether the grandparents are awarded custody of the child is something in the providence of the Judge hearing the case.

#80: No Provision for Siblings

What about the rights of siblings to future contact with a child placed for adoption with a non-relative? In the case of a newborn child placed for private adoption, there is no provision in the law for the child's siblings to have access to the adopted sibling and the issue usually comes into play when a group of older siblings is placed for adoption, generally due to abuse or neglect by their parents. The states try to keep siblings together when appropriate. That said, there are few guarantees that siblings will be kept together or that they will have contact with each other as they grow up.

#81: Future Contact Can Come In Many Different Varieties

Post-placement contact between the adoptive family and the birth parents can take many forms. We have participated in situations ranging from the exchange of pictures and updates all the way up to meetings at Disney World years after the adoption. We know of families who regularly speak, e-mail and Skype with the birth parents of their adopted child(ren).

There is no right or wrong, it's only a matter of what the parties mutually agree upon based on their comfort levels. While many families have an emotional fear of the birth parents "coming back" and wanting to reclaim custody of the child, this fear is not generally supported by logic. Once communication starts and both sides realize that the others aren't a two-headed monster, life-long friendships and relationships can develop.

On the other hand, we have also seen future contact degenerate into pleas for money or 'loans' to the birth parents, who are still trying to 'get back on their feet.' There are certain types of people who will always be in need of help from others due to their bad decision-making and/or lifestyle choices. Your adoption professional should guide you towards making the decision that's best for you and your family.

CHAPTER 10

ADOPTION MISCELLANY

#82: Support Groups Available

Support groups for adoption issues of all kinds are available, and there are very likely several in or near your area. There are support groups for adoptees, birth mothers, adoptive parents, adoptive parents of special needs kids, and almost every other category of adoption-related issue you can think of. The best way to find this information is through an internet search. Literally, just search for "adoption support groups" and add your geographic location, and you'll be amazed at the world of opportunities you'll have to connect with others in similar situations.

Sometimes families who have had one or more bad adoption experiences feel like the cards are stacked against them. They sometimes become hopeless and desperate, which puts them in a delicate position wherein they can be preyed upon even further by unscrupulous adoption entities (legal or illegal) and/or adoption fraudsters. Membership and participation in an adoption support group can mitigate some or all of the negative feelings and allow the family to move on in whatever direction they choose.

#83: Safe Haven

In Florida, a birth mother (or birth father) may anonymously leave a baby who is approximately 7 days of age at a fire station, hospital or police station (a "safe haven") and not be criminally prosecuted for such action. No identification of either birth parent is required. However, if a baby appears to be abused or neglected, the law will attempt to pursue the parents and prosecute them for any one or more of a variety of crimes including child abuse and neglect.

Safe Haven laws are in response to those rare cases where a woman has a baby that she does not want or about which she was in denial, and does something horrific with the baby to conceal the fact that it was born.

Beware of private entities calling themselves "Safe Haven." Use of that term does not necessarily mean that the entity is an official or governmental entity at all.

#84: "Safe Haven" Child Placed with Licensed Agency

A child left at a safe haven must be taken to a hospital (unless the hospital is the safe haven) and a representative of the hospital must contact a state licensed child placing agency (i.e., adoption agency) for the purposes of making the child available for adoption through such agency.

The good news about "Safe Haven" baby adoptions is that the family that is selected to adopt the baby is relieved of the usual roller coaster ride associated with a much longer waiting period. The bad news is that there is really no history of what, if any, pre-natal care the birth mother has had, or what her physical, mental, medical, drug, or family history is. The only information is derived from the pediatric examination of the baby. Obviously a drug test is done and a full panel of pediatric testing is performed, but no history is available because the identity of the birth parents is unknown.

Another negative feature is that unlike a conventional adoption wherein the birth mother's consent is irrevocable after it is given, the birth mother in a "Safe Haven" placement may surface at any time before her parental rights are terminated and attempt to reclaim the baby. This can easily add 30-60 days to the period during which the adoption can be upset.

Neither the hospital, fire station nor police department where a Safe Haven baby is left is charged with making the adoptive placement. That responsibility is for a licensed child-placing agency which may place the child for adoption without the identity or consent of either of the birth parents.

In the case of a Safe Haven adoption, a birth mother may, at any time prior to the termination of her parental rights in court, return and attempt to regain custody of the child.

#85: No Grandparental Rights

In Florida, grandparents have no "right of first refusal" to adopt a grandchild if the child's mother wants to place the child for adoption. Grandparents may be entitled to receive notice of a pending adoption, but only if the child has lived with them for a period of 6 months or more during the 24 months preceding the filing of a petition to terminate parental rights of the birth parents. If the child has lived with them for the required time period, they must be given notice of the final hearing of adoption and the opportunity to convince the Judge that it is in the child's best interests that they adopt the child.

#86: Lack of Uniformity in Adoption Laws State-to-State

An adoption that may be perfectly legal and legitimate in one state could easily be the opposite in another. While there are a handful of national acts or compacts (i.e., ICWA and ICPC) that are fairly uniform across the country, the rules as to how adoptions are handled in any given state are literally up to the whim of that state's legislature at any given time.

The Florida legislature has been relatively consistent over time in taking its cues from the professional adoption community insofar as what the rules ought to be in order for there to be a fair balance between the rights of the baby, the birth mother, the adoptive family, and the father. Some large special interests have attempted to insinuate themselves into the process, but the outcome of the legislative process was a fair but not perfect set of laws.

#87: Judges Have the Final Say-So

Since adoptions are creatures of state laws, Judges are responsible for interpreting and applying such laws to the facts presented to them in each case. Regardless of how many 't's are crossed and 'I's are dotted, if a Judge doesn't believe that the adoption is in the best interest of the child, it isn't going to happen. Thus, the review of all legally required documents in-cluding the home study and other background information is an essential piece of the adoption puzzle for which a Judge is responsible.

#88: Transition of Older Child

While the transition of an infant into an adoptive home is usually a fairly smooth process, the transition of an older child presents an entirely different set of challenges which should be addressed between and among the prospective adoptive family, the social worker, and the adoption professional well before the process is undertaken. Special counseling and training of the adoptive family is always a preferred method of approaching the older child adoption process.

> *Case in point:* *In a recent case, our social worker advised a family that was adopting an older child that there is generally a "honeymoon period" during which the child often tests the limits which the family will permit. This older child had "issues" and "baggage", meant respectfully, and the adoptive family would not know the depth or breadth of those issues until the child knew the permanency, security, and stability of his new family. Our social worker counseled them that only when those goals are attained would the child's true personality emerge thus enabling the family to focus on which specific needs required attention.*

> *Having followed the advice given, particularly the emphasis on developing a sense of permanency, security, and stability, the family appears to have the situation under control and a naive observer would never*

know that this family had not been together forever.

#89: Adjustment of Child from Foreign Country

The adjustment of a child adopted from a foreign country presents an entirely different process of adjustment. Depending on age and language skills, the transition may require additional educational, counseling cultural and linguistic attention. Fortunately, there are vast resources available on-line to help with the transition. Further, with the rising number of these types of adoption has come increasing numbers of professionals on the local level with training and experience in the issues unique to these adoptions.

#90: Black Market Adoptions

The limited number of children available for adoption versus the much greater number of prospective adoptive families has created what is generally referred to as a "black market" for babies. The "black market" typically consists of unscrupulous lawyers, birth parents, facilitators, agencies and others seeking to essentially sell babies to the highest bidders. Laws, ethics, and morality take a back seat to the almighty dollar. Once again, an experienced adoption profes- sional can help you avoid getting involved in an illegal adoption situation.

Furthermore, if a prospective adoptive family has to go to an unscrupulous "baby broker" or "black marketeer" to adopt a baby, there's probably a really good reason they can't do so legally or the traditional way. Birth mothers who place babies for adoption in exchange for cold, hard cash need to ask themselves why these people have to resort to this type of situation in order to adopt.

Since fraud is at the center of so-called "black market" adoptions, the validity of a resulting adoption decree is always highly dubious and may cause the adoption to be set aside if there is a challenge.

CHAPTER 11

SURROGACY AND PRE-PLANNED ADOPTION

#91: Surrogacy is an Adoption-Related Solution

Surrogacy is an adoption-related solution to some couples' infertility issues. Surrogacy is, generally speaking, more expensive than adoption, but offers more protection against fraud, scams, or honest-to-god changes of mind.

#92: Gestational vs. Traditional Surrogacy

Some couples choose to hire a woman to carry their own biological child for them. When the embryo is completely unrelated to the couple, this process is called "gestational surrogacy." When the surrogate is artificially inseminated using the surrogate's own egg, the process is called "traditional surrogacy."

No one in their right mind would engage themselves or anyone they know in a "traditional surrogacy" for a variety of legal reasons. Traditional surrogacy is fraught with legal, social, and moral peril. For example, if the surrogate chooses not to relinquish the child, the donor of the sperm, who is often the husband in the commissioning couple, could be sued for 18 years of child support. We would not advise our clients to undertake a traditional surrogacy unless the gestational surrogate was a very close relative of one of the intended parents. Even then we would probably advise against it. It's just too socially, emotionally, and financially risky.

#93: Florida's Progressive Surrogacy Laws

Florida has extremely progressive laws in the area of surrogacy. Surrogacy is very expensive, but the good news is that Florida and some other states have laws that make the legalities of the process very straightforward.

The straightforwardness of Florida surrogacy laws is based on the fact that there is a clearly written and well-though-out statute that takes into account the rights of the various parties. The statute also calls for written agreements which clearly outline the rights and responsibilities, and risks and rewards. The law further permits the surrogate a reasonable financial reimbursement for the costs she incurs during the process. There is a higher likelihood that a doctor will order bed rest or that a surrogate will miss work during the process, due in part to the fact that many surrogacy pregnancies create multiple fetuses. These matters are taken into account by Florida law.

It's no accident that the law is as well-written as it is; it's the product of a great deal of work by the Florida legislature and the professionals who practice in the area of surrogacy every day.

#94: Surrogates Are Screened Differently than Birth Mothers

Surrogates are screened very differently than birth mothers in adoption. While birth mothers in adoption are already pregnant at the time they contact the agency, and are therefore subject to a sort of 'come as you are' analysis, a prospective surrogate must undergo fairly rigorous medical and psychological screening in order to be accepted into a surrogacy program. Essentially, she is "vetted" by the surrogacy agency or attorney, the IVF doctor and the intended parent(s). The screening should include a psychological examination by a mental health professional who is familiar and experienced with the specific issues brought on by the surrogacy process.

Even seemingly perfectly qualified surrogacy candidates can be disqualified from the process by issues such as slightly elevated blood pressure or BMI (body mass index).

Case in Point: Jeannette and Jeff run a surrogacy agency called Life Through

Surrogacy, Inc.[4] in which we assist surrogates and intended parent(s) in the gestational surrogacy or pre-planned adoption processes.

We received an inquiry over the website from a woman named Cindy who wanted to be a gestational carrier. She was physically and psychologically healthy, and wanted to have her living expenses paid while at the same time providing the gift of a child to a family who couldn't carry for themselves. Cindy sounded like a very nice person, so we arranged to meet with her.

Cindy presented herself as appropriately mature for her age of 34, intelligent and thoughtful, and an excellent parent to her eight-year-old child. She appeared to be stable, with a good job and clean living situation. So far as we could tell, we loved Cindy.

We sent Cindy to a psychological exam which resulted in a recommendation by the psychologist that Cindy be approved as a gestational surrogate. The last piece of the

---

[4] Life Through Surrogacy, Inc.
http://www.LifeThroughSurrogacy.com

puzzle was the physical exam by the IVF physician.

The report from the IVF physician's exam showed that Cindy was a perfect candidate for surrogacy in every area except for one: her BMI. At 5'4", Cindy's weight should have been from 101 to 145 lbs., according to the National Institutes of Health's body mass index calculations. At her weight of 158, Cindy was considered "overweight" and, believe it or not, borderline "obese"! As a consequence of her weight issue, Cindy also had a slightly elevated blood pressure.

If this were anyone else, it would be no big deal. Cindy didn't exactly look skinny but one wouldn't look at her and consider her borderline obese! Cindy looked healthy. However, due to the fairly stringent BMI factors considered by the medical professionals, Cindy was provisionally rejected. The provision obviously was based on her weight. If she lost 13 or more pounds she would be reconsidered.

One of the thousand reasons I love working with Jeannette is that she is a female and is much better suited than I to tell a female that she is overweight. Cindy took the news very well and told us that she had been thinking about dropping a few pounds anyway, and this news was the exact motivation she needed. Let's face it, the living expenses in surrogacy can be fairly generous, and that kind of help can be pretty effective motivation when you're looking for a bit of leverage over yourself.

Jeannette and Cindy kept in touch over the next few months, and Cindy kept Jeannette apprised on her efforts to drop a few pounds. Four months later, Cindy had her re-evaluation appointment. Her BMI had dropped to within acceptable range and her blood pressure was average. Thus a match was made, and as this small piece is written Cindy is in the process of her new chapter in life as a gestational surrogate!

#95: Gestational Surrogate Cannot Keep Baby

A gestational surrogate cannot legally change her mind and keep the baby. Unlike adoption, the surrogate is carrying the child which belongs, almost in a property-type right, to the couple who commissioned the pregnancy. The number one concern in the typical adoption case is that the birth mother will keep the baby and choose to parent instead of place. This concern does not exist in gestational surrogacy.

#96: Commissioning Couple Must Be Married

In order for a surrogacy to comply with Florida surrogacy law, the "commissioning couple" or "intended parents" must be a married couple. Further, the embryos used in the in-vitro fertilization must be biologically related to one or both members of the couple.

If the case does not fall into the above criteria, it can be done as a pre-planned adoption. A pre-planned adoption under Florida law offers similar protections as a surrogacy, but is a little ambiguous on a the key issue of whether the gestational carrier has the right to cancel the contract with the intended parent(s) at any time. This glitch will hopefully be cleared up by the Florida legislature.

#97: Selective Reduction

The important moral issue of "selective reduction" comes up in surrogacy. That issue includes how many embryos ought to be implanted, and what to do about a multiple pregnancy should one occur.

The number of embryos to implant is a decision for the doctor, the intended parents and the surrogate. If multiple embryos are implanted and a multiple pregnancy occurs, the issue of "selective reduction" arises. "Selective reduction" refers to the destruction or abortion of what might be perfectly healthy fetuses. This needs to be addressed by the couple well in advance of moving forward with surrogacy or pre-planned adoption.

#98: Leftover Embryos

Suppose you've accomplished a successful surrogacy or pre-planned adoption . . . . Congratulations! Now, what do you do with the leftover embryos?

Some people believe that the destruction of viable embryos is the taking of a human life. Some people believe that they can make a difference by donating embryos for scientific research, while for others that is completely unacceptable. Some people choose to give the leftover embryos away to other couples who will use them for their own attempts at parenthood. Some people will allow their embryos to sit in the fertility clinic's facilities until they age-out, essentially "dying" of natural causes.

All of the above choices are right and wrong, depending on who you are. These are issues that will come up and must be addressed with the professionals who will be helping you in this process.

#99: Parenthood Is Awesome, Good Luck

Last but not least . . . . Parenthood is awesome! It has challenges, risks, & rewards. After reading this list if you're still interested in taking the huge step towards adoption or surrogacy, we encourage . . . no, we URGE . . . you to ask questions, LOTS OF QUESTIONS, to adoption professionals and people in your area who have been successful in adoption. Go into this process with eyes wide open, and prepare to risk it all.

We wish you the best of luck in your journey towards parenthood!

APPENDIX A:

WORKSHEETS

Notes to Self:

Notes to Self:

Notes to Self:

Notes to Self:

Notes to Self:

Notes to Self:

APPENDIX B:

GLOSSARY OF TERMS

The following terms are used in the preceding pages. The definitions listed below are not 100% legally accurate and all-encompassing, and are not necessarily the legal definitions used in every jurisdiction. They reflect the meaning we are giving to them as used in this colloquial non-legal text.

Adoption: the legal process of creating a legal parent/child relationship where one did not exist. The adoptee may be a child or an adult.

Adoption Entity: a validly-licensed adoption services provider in any given jurisdiction. For example, can be a licensed agency or attorney.

Adoption Facilitator: an unlicensed person who helps with adoptions. Not legal in every jurisdiction (i.e., Florida).

Adoption Professional: see adoption entity.

Adoption Reunion Registry: state-maintained database whose purpose is to reunite birth parents with adopted children in a legally prescribed manner.

Birth Mother: a woman who is planning to, expected to, or has placed a baby for adoption.

Child: the subject of a prospective adoption; may be as-yet unborn.

Closed Adoption: means different things to different people. Generally refers to the degree of pre- and/or post-birth contact that a birth parent and adoptive parent will have. There is no such thing as "open" or "closed" adoption in the laws of many states. In a "closed" adoption, there would be little or no contact between birth and adoptive parents.

Commissioning Couple: a couple who creates embryos and engages a surrogate to carry one or more babies for them via a legal surrogacy process.

Consent: the legal permission to place a person for adoption, given by the party from whom the rights are to be transferred.

Degree of Consanguinity: the degree to which two people are related by blood.

Duress: use of force or stress, in this case in order to force or induce one to sign a Consent against his/her will.

Fathers:

- Biological—the actual biological father of a person.
- Birth—usually refers to biological father.
- Legal—a man who was married to a woman at any time during her pregnancy, regardless as to whether that man is the biological father of the child.
- Putative—someone claiming to be or alleging to be the biological father of a person.
- Unmarried Biological—the biological father of a child when that man is not married to the mother.

Financial Support: legally-permitted and sometimes court-ordered assistance to a birth mother for her permissible living expenses.

Fraud: illegal deception (i.e., lying) for the purpose of some type of gain, financial or otherwise

Home Study: a thorough and detailed report written by one licensed to do so (often a social worker) detailing the life and history of a prospective adoptive home. Required by law in every state and in most adoptions. Includes criminal background information, reference letters, financial, educational, occupational, and other significant areas of and influences on the lives of the prospective adoptive family.

ICPC: Interstate Compact on the Placement of Children—a compact between all 50 states setting out the rules through which children can legally travel from one state to another for purposes of adoption.

ICWA: Indian Child Welfare Act—a federal law that seeks to keep Indian (Native American) children with Indian families.

Intended Parent(s): see "Commissioning couple," can also be used in connection with pre-planned adoption.

Open Adoption: means different things to different people. Generally refers to the degree of pre- and/or post-birth contact that a birth parent and adoptive parent will have. There is no such thing as "open" or "closed" adoption in the laws of many states. In an "open" adoption there would be a higher degree of contact between birth and adoptive parents.

Pre-planned Adoption: similar to surrogacy, but can include singles or unmarried couples, and commissioned pregnancies in which the intended parent(s) have no biological relationship to the child.

Revocation (or Withdrawal) Period: the period after placement of a child for adoption during which the placing parent(s) would be legally permitted to cancel the adoption and regain custody of the child. Florida does not have a revocation period for children under six months of age.

Selective Reduction: the medical termination or abortion of a fetus, usually during a surrogacy or pre-planned pregnancy, due to the multiplicity of the pregnancy and/or the health of one or more of the fetuses.

Special Needs: special legally-enumerated reasons that a child might get subsidy and/or special treatment under the law. Includes special medical/mental/emotional needs, sibling group, ethnic minority, etc.

Step-Parent Adoption: legal adoption of a person by a person unrelated to them while preserving the legal rights of person who has legal custody or rights over the adoptee. May require marriage to the legal parent, but depending on the state can be done via domestic partnership or civil union.

Surrogacy: *Gestational*—placement of embryo(s) into the uterus of a "carrier" who is not biologically related to the embryo(s). *Traditional*—artificial insemination, or in-vitro implantation, of an embryo into the uterus of a "carrier" when the carrier's egg is used to create the embryo. ***NOT RECOMMENDED***

Subsidy: financial assistance, usually governmental, for the adoption and/or care of a child, usually in connection with special needs or a difficult placement.

Waiting Period: the time between the birth of a child and the time when the adoption consent can be legally given.

ABOUT THE AUTHORS

Robert A. Kasky, Esq. is a
Florida lawyer, co-founder
and President of One World
Adoption Services, Inc., a
Florida-licensed not-for-profit child placing agency.
Robert began his legal career
as the Earth was cooling, way
back in 1966 as an attorney for the SEC in
Washington D.C. Robert is a Florida Supreme
Court Certified Circuit Civil Mediator,
completed his first adoption in 1973 and has
since handled or worked on thousands of
adoption cases. He has also served as and is
available as a mediator and an expert witness in
adoption cases.

Jeffrey A. Kasky, Esq. is also a Florida lawyer and is co-founder and Vice President of One World Adoption Services, Inc., a Florida-licensed not-for-profit child placing agency. Jeff is currently a  Florida-certified law enforcement officer, a Florida Supreme Court Certified Mediator in Circuit, County, and Family Courts, and has been practicing law for the adoption agency since it opened in 1995. Jeff has also acted in numerous cases as a volunteer guardian ad litem for abused and/or neglected children in the Broward County Dependency Court. Prior to that, Jeff spent three law school years clerking for Robert, working on adoption cases. Jeff has also served as and is available as a mediator and an expert witness in adoption cases.

Available Titles in the 99 Series®

99 Things You Wish You Knew Before . . .
Facing a Bully
Facing Life's Challenges
Going to Culinary School
Landing Your Dream Job
Losing Fat 4 Life
Making It BIG In Media
Marketing on the Internet
Mobile Device was Hacked
Stressing Out!
Your Identity Was Stolen

99 Things Women Wish They Knew Before . . .
Dating After 40, 50, and YES, 60!
Falling in Love
Getting Behind the Wheel of Their Dream Job
Getting Fit Without Hitting the Gym
Planning for Retirement
Saying "I Do"
Servicing Their Car
Starting Their Own Business

99 Things -
Parents Wish They Knew Before Having
"THE" Talk
Brides Wish They Knew Before Planning
Their Wedding
Teens Wish They Knew Before Turning 16

http://www.99-Series.com